Cram101 Textbook Outlines to accompany:

Clinical Psychology

Trull, 7th Edition

An Academic Internet Publishers (AIPI) publication (c) 2007.

You have a discounted membership at www.Cram101.com with this book.

Get all of the practice tests for the chapters of this textbook, and access in-depth reference material for writing essays and papers. Here is an example from a Cram101 Biology text:

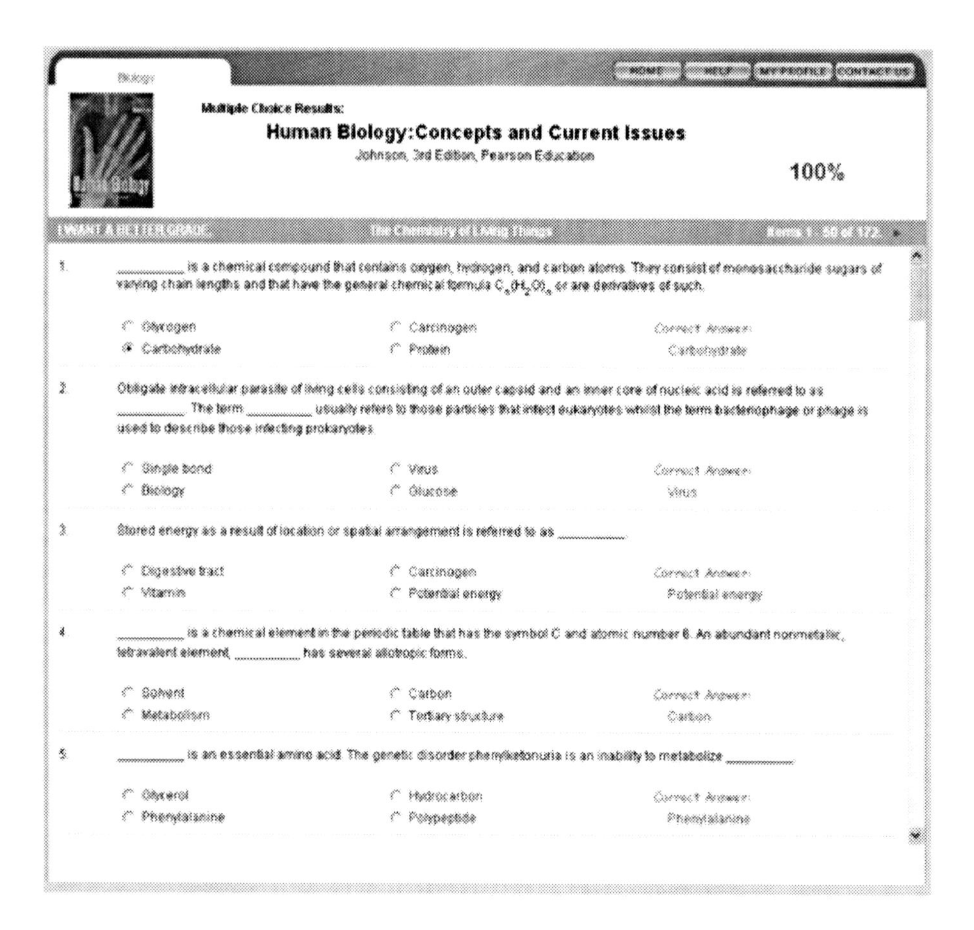

When you need problem solving help with math, stats, and other disciplines, www.Cram101.com will walk through the formulas and solutions step by step.

With Cram101.com online, you also have access to extensive reference material.

You will nail those essays and papers. Here is an example from a Cram101 Biology text:

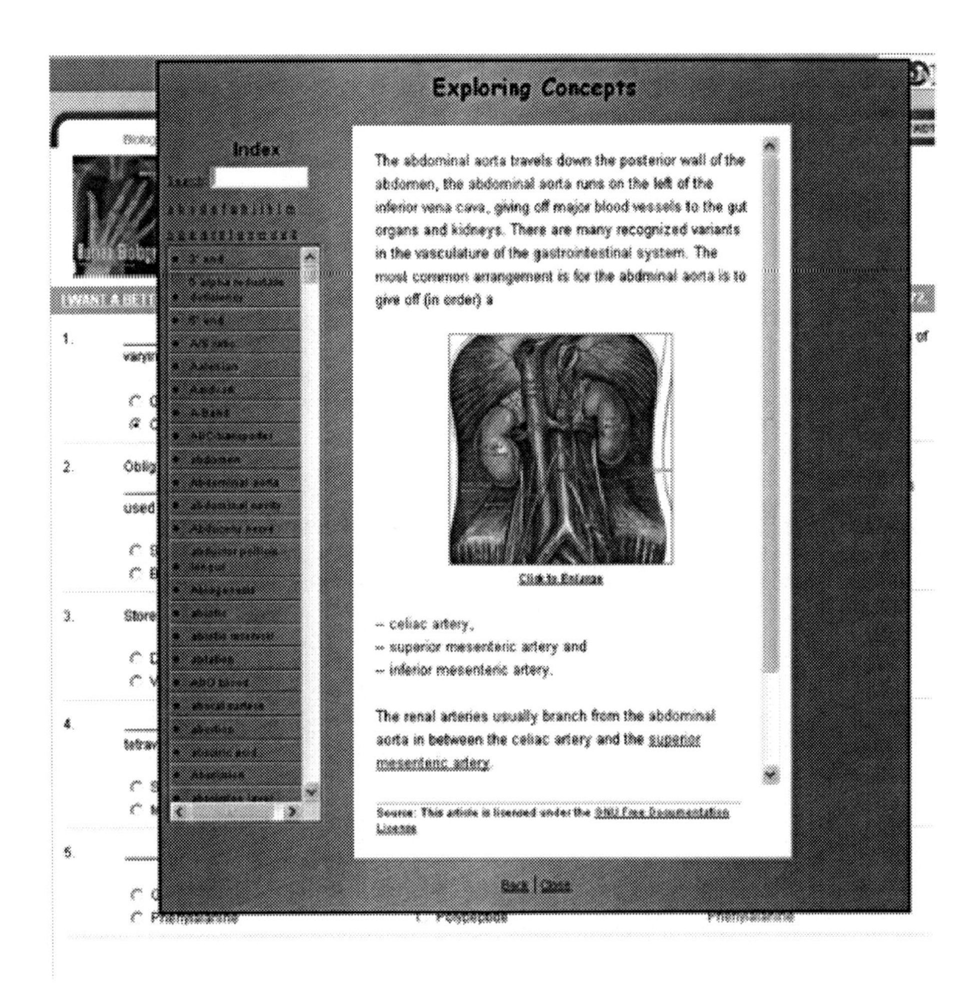

Visit **www.Cram101.com**, click Sign Up at the top of the screen, and enter DK73DW3606 in the promo code box on the registration screen. Access to www.Cram101.com is normally $9.95, but because you have purchased this book, your access fee is only $4.95. Sign up and stop highlighting textbooks forever.

Learning System

Cram101 Textbook Outlines is a learning system. The notes in this book are the highlights of your textbook, you will never have to highlight a book again.

How to use this book. Take this book to class, it is your notebook for the lecture. The notes and highlights on the left hand side of the pages follow the outline and order of the textbook. All you have to do is follow along while your intructor presents the lecture. Circle the items emphasized in class and add other important information on the right side. With Cram101 Textbook Outlines you'll spend less time writing and more time listening. Learning becomes more efficient.

Cram101.com Online

Increase your studying efficiency by using Cram101.com's practice tests and online reference material. It is the perfect complement to Cram101 Textbook Outlines. Use self-teaching matching tests or simulate in-class testing with comprehensive multiple choice tests, or simply use Cram's true and false tests for quick review. Cram101.com even allows you to enter your in-class notes for an integrated studying format combining the textbook notes with your class notes.

Visit **www.Cram101.com**, click Sign Up at the top of the screen, and enter **DK73DW3606** in the promo code box on the registration screen. Access to www.Cram101.com is normally $9.95, but because you have purchased this book, your access fee is only $4.95. Sign up and stop highlighting textbooks forever.

 ISBN: 1-4288-1318-7

Clinical Psychology
Trull, 7th

CONTENTS

Heterogeneous	A heterogeneous compound, mixture, or other such object is one that consists of many different items, which are often not easily sorted or separated, though they are clearly distinct.
Clinical psychologist	A psychologist, usually with a Ph.D, whose training is in the diagnosis, treatment, or research of psychological and behavioral disorders is a clinical psychologist.
Psychoanalysis	Psychoanalysis refers to the school of psychology that emphasizes the importance of unconscious motives and conflicts as determinants of human behavior. It was Freud's method of exploring human personality.
Clinical psychology	Clinical psychology is involved in the diagnosis, assessment, and treatment of patients with mental or behavioral disorders, and conducts research in these various areas.
Society	The social sciences use the term society to mean a group of people that form a semi-closed (or semi-open) social system, in which most interactions are with other individuals belonging to the group.
Psychopathology	Psychopathology refers to the field concerned with the nature and development of mental disorders.
Personality	Personality refers to the pattern of enduring characteristics that differentiates a person, the patterns of behaviors that make each individual unique.
Socioeconomic	Socioeconomic pertains to the study of the social and economic impacts of any product or service offering, market intervention or other activity on an economy as a whole and on the companies, organization and individuals who are its main economic actors.
Life span	Life span refers to the upper boundary of life, the maximum number of years an individual can live. The maximum life span of human beings is about 120 years of age. Females live an average of 6 years longer than males.
Clinician	A health professional authorized to provide services to people suffering from one or more pathologies is a clinician.
Counseling psychology	Counseling psychology is unique in its attention both to normal developmental issues and to problems associated with physical, emotional, and mental disorders.
Psychoanalytic	Freud's theory that unconscious forces act as determinants of personality is called psychoanalytic theory. The theory is a developmental theory characterized by critical stages of development.
Psychiatrist	A psychiatrist is a physician who specializes in the diagnosis and treatment of psychological disorders.
Psychotherapy	Psychotherapy is a set of techniques based on psychological principles intended to improve mental health, emotional or behavioral issues.
Research method	The scope of the research method is to produce some new knowledge. This, in principle, can take three main forms: Exploratory research; Constructive research; and Empirical research.
Scientific research	Research that is objective, systematic, and testable is called scientific research.
Survey	A method of scientific investigation in which a large sample of people answer questions about their attitudes or behavior is referred to as a survey.
Ethnic group	An ethnic group is a culture or subculture whose members are readily distinguishable by outsiders based on traits originating from a common racial, national, linguistic, or religious source. Members of an ethnic group are often presumed to be culturally or biologically similar, although this is not in fact necessarily the case.
Counseling psychologist	A doctoral level mental health professional whose training is similar to that of a clinical psychologist, though usually with less emphasis on research and serious psychopathology is referred to as a counseling psychologist.
Autonomy	Autonomy is the condition of something that does not depend on anything else.

Authoritarian	The term authoritarian is used to describe a style that enforces strong and sometimes oppressive measures against those in its sphere of influence, generally without attempts at gaining their consent.
Social learning	Social learning is learning that occurs as a function of observing, retaining and replicating behavior observed in others. Although social learning can occur at any stage in life, it is thought to be particularly important during childhood, particularly as authority becomes important.
Learning	Learning is a relatively permanent change in behavior that results from experience. Thus, to attribute a behavioral change to learning, the change must be relatively permanent and must result from experience.
Biofeedback	Biofeedback is the process of measuring and quantifying an aspect of a subject's physiology, analyzing the data, and then feeding back the information to the subject in a form that allows the subject to enact physiological change.
Health psychology	The field of psychology that studies the relationships between psychological factors and the prevention and treatment of physical illness is called health psychology.
Psychological disorder	Mental processes and/or behavior patterns that cause emotional distress and/or substantial impairment in functioning is a psychological disorder.
American Psychological Association	The American Psychological Association is a professional organization representing psychology in the US. The mission statement is to "advance psychology as a science and profession and as a means of promoting health, education , and human welfare".
Psychiatric social worker	A mental health professional trained to apply social science principles to help patients in clinics and hospitals is the psychiatric social worker.
Family therapy	Family therapy is a branch of psychotherapy that treats family problems. Family therapists consider the family as a system of interacting members; as such, the problems in the family are seen to arise as an emergent property of the interactions in the system, rather than ascribed exclusively to the "faults" or psychological problems of individual members.
Social psychology	Social psychology is the study of the nature and causes of human social behavior, with an emphasis on how people think towards each other and how they relate to each other.
Occupational therapists	Occupational therapists work with the disabled, the elderly, newborns, school-aged children, and with anyone who has a permanent or temporary impairment in their physical or mental functioning.
Social skills	Social skills are skills used to interact and communicate with others to assist status in the social structure and other motivations.
Paraprofessional	A paraprofessional is an individual lacking a doctoral degree but trained to perform certain functions usually reserved for clinicians.
Depression	In everyday language depression refers to any downturn in mood, which may be relatively transitory and perhaps due to something trivial. This is differentiated from Clinical depression which is marked by symptoms that last two weeks or more and are so severe that they interfere with daily living.
Addiction	Addiction is an uncontrollable compulsion to repeat a behavior regardless of its consequences. Many drugs or behaviors can precipitate a pattern of conditions recognized as addiction, which include a craving for more of the drug or behavior, increased physiological tolerance to exposure, and withdrawal symptoms in the absence of the stimulus.
Psychosis	Psychosis is a generic term for mental states in which the components of rational thought and perception are severely impaired. Persons experiencing a psychosis may experience hallucinations, hold paranoid or delusional beliefs, demonstrate personality changes and exhibit disorganized thinking. This is usually accompanied by features such as a lack of insight into the unusual or bizarre nature of their behavior, difficulties with social interaction and impairments in carrying out the activities of daily living.

Anxiety	Anxiety is a complex combination of the feeling of fear, apprehension and worry often accompanied by physical sensations such as palpitations, chest pain and/or shortness of breath.
Juvenile delinquency	Juvenile delinquency refers to a broad range of child and adolescent behaviors, including socially unacceptable behavior, status offenses, and criminal acts.
Personality disorder	A mental disorder characterized by a set of inflexible, maladaptive personality traits that keep a person from functioning properly in society is referred to as a personality disorder.
Learning disability	A learning disability exists when there is a significant discrepancy between one's ability and achievement.
Mental retardation	Mental retardation refers to having significantly below-average intellectual functioning and limitations in at least two areas of adaptive functioning. Many categorize retardation as mild, moderate, severe, or profound.
Questionnaire	A self-report method of data collection or clinical assessment method in which the individual being studied checks off items on a printed list, answers multiple-choice questions, or writes out answers to essay questions aimed at producing a selfdescription is called questionnaire.
Random sample	A sample drawn so that each member of a population has an equal chance of being selected to participate is referred to as a random sample.
Group therapy	Group therapy is a form of psychotherapy during which one or several therapists treat a small group of clients together as a group. This may be more cost effective than individual therapy, and possibly even more effective.
Insight	Insight refers to a sudden awareness of the relationships among various elements that had previously appeared to be independent of one another.
Personality test	A personality test aims to describe aspects of a person's character that remain stable across situations.
Child abuse	Child abuse is the physical or psychological maltreatment of a child.
Psychological testing	Psychological testing is a field characterized by the use of small samples of behavior in order to infer larger generalizations about a given individual. The technical term for psychological testing is psychometrics.
Abnormal psychology	The scientific study whose objectives are to describe, explain, predict, and control behaviors that are considered strange or unusual is referred to as abnormal psychology.
Mental disorder	Mental disorder refers to a disturbance in a person's emotions, drives, thought processes, or behavior that involves serious and relatively prolonged distress and/or impairment in ability to function, is not simply a normal response to some event or set of events in the person's environment.
Drug addiction	Drug addiction, or substance dependence is the compulsive use of drugs, to the point where the user has no effective choice but to continue use.
Relapse prevention	Extending therapeutic progress by teaching the client how to cope with future troubling situations is a relapse prevention technique.
Cognitive therapy	Cognitive therapy is a kind of psychotherapy used to treat depression, anxiety disorders, phobias, and other forms of mental disorder. It involves recognizing distorted thinking and learning how to replace it with more realistic thoughts and actions.
Substance abuse	Substance abuse refers to the overindulgence in and dependence on a stimulant, depressant, or other chemical substance, leading to effects that are detrimental to the individual's physical or mental health, or the welfare of others.
Social support	Social Support is the physical and emotional comfort given by family, friends, co-workers and others. Research has identified three main types of social support: emotional, practical, sharing points of

view.

Comorbidity — Comorbidity refers to the presence of more than one mental disorder occurring in an individual at the same time.

Alcoholic — An alcoholic is dependent on alcohol as characterized by craving, loss of control, physical dependence and withdrawal symptoms, and tolerance.

Arthritis — Arthritis is a group of conditions that affect the health of the bone joints in the body. Arthritis can be caused from strains and injuries caused by repetitive motion, sports, overexertion, and falls. Unlike the autoimmune diseases, it largely affects older people and results from the degeneration of joint cartilage.

Pathology — Pathology is the study of the processes underlying disease and other forms of illness, harmful abnormality, or dysfunction.

Trauma — Trauma refers to a severe physical injury or wound to the body caused by an external force, or a psychological shock having a lasting effect on mental life.

Alcohol use disorders — Cognitive, biological, behavioral, and social problems associated with alcohol use and abuse are referred to as alcohol use disorders.

Pathological gambling — Pathological gambling, as defined by American Psychiatric Association is an impulse control disorder associated with gambling. It is a chronic and progresive mental illness. It is estimated that 4-6% of gamblers are subject to the disease and that adolescents are three times more susceptible than adults.

Alcoholics Anonymous — The primary purpose of Alcoholics Anonymous membership is to stay sober and help others do the same. It. formed the original twelve-step program and has been the source and model for all similar recovery groups.

Longitudinal study — Longitudinal study is a type of developmental study in which the same group of participants is followed and measured for an extended period of time, often years.

Psychodynamic — Most psychodynamic approaches are centered around the idea of a maladapted function developed early in life (usually childhood) which are at least in part unconscious. This maladapted function (a.k.a. defense mechanism) does not do well in place of a normal/healthy one.

Maladaptive — In psychology, a behavior or trait is adaptive when it helps an individual adjust and function well within their social environment. A maladaptive behavior or trait is counterproductive to the individual.

Intelligence test — An intelligence test is a standardized means of assessing a person's current mental ability, for example, the Stanford-Binet test and the Wechsler Adult Intelligence Scale.

Projective test — A projective test is a personality test designed to let a person respond to ambiguous stimuli, presumably revealing hidden emotions and internal conflicts. This is different from an "objective test" in which responses are analyzed according to a universal standard rather than an individual psychiatrist's judgement.

Psychological test — Psychological test refers to a standardized measure of a sample of a person's behavior.

Token economy — An environmental setting that fosters desired behavior by reinforcing it with tokens that can be exchanged for other reinforcers is called a token economy.

Habit — A habit is a response that has become completely separated from its eliciting stimulus. Early learning theorists used the term to describe S-R associations, however not all S-R associations become a habit, rather many are extinguished after reinforcement is withdrawn.

Prototype — A concept of a category of objects or events that serves as a good example of the category is called a prototype.

Individual differences	Individual differences psychology studies the ways in which individual people differ in their behavior. This is distinguished from other aspects of psychology in that although psychology is ostensibly a study of individuals, modern psychologists invariably study groups.
Affect	A subjective feeling or emotional tone often accompanied by bodily expressions noticeable to others is called affect.
Nomothetic	Nomothetic measures are contrasted to ipsative or idiothetic measures, where nomothetic measures are measures that can be taken directly by an outside observer, such as weight or how many times a particular behavior occurs, and ipsative measures are self-reports such as a rank-ordered list of preferences.
Principles of Behavior	Hull published Principles of Behavior, in 1943. His theory is characterized by very strict operationalization of variables and mathematical presentation. The essence of the theory can be summarized by saying that the response is a function of the strength of the habit times the strength of the drive. It is for this reason that Hull's theory is often referred to as drive theory.
Intuition	Quick, impulsive thought that does not make use of formal logic or clear reasoning is referred to as intuition.
Homogeneous	In biology homogeneous has a meaning similar to its meaning in mathematics. Generally it means "the same" or "of the same quality or general property".
Dichotomy	A dichotomy is the division of a proposition into two parts which are both mutually exclusive – i.e. both cannot be simultaneously true – and jointly exhaustive – i.e. they cover the full range of possible outcomes. They are often contrasting and spoken of as "opposites".
Reliability	Reliability means the extent to which a test produces a consistent , reproducible score .
Empirical	Empirical means the use of working hypotheses which are capable of being disproved using observation or experiment.
Validity	The extent to which a test measures what it is intended to measure is called validity.
Resurgence	Resurgence refers to the reappearance during extinction, of a previously reinforced behavior.
Statistics	Statistics is a type of data analysis which practice includes the planning, summarizing, and interpreting of observations of a system possibly followed by predicting or forecasting of future events based on a mathematical model of the system being observed.
Statistic	A statistic is an observable random variable of a sample.
Research design	A research design tests a hypothesis. The basic typess are: descriptive, correlational, and experimental.
Developmental psychology	The branch of psychology that studies the patterns of growth and change occurring throughout life is referred to as developmental psychology.
Cognitive psychology	Cognitive psychology is the psychological science which studies the mental processes that are hypothesised to underlie behavior. This covers a broad range of research domains, examining questions about the workings of memory, attention, perception, knowledge representation, reasoning, creativity and problem solving.
Schizophrenia	Schizophrenia is characterized by persistent defects in the perception or expression of reality. A person suffering from untreated schizophrenia typically demonstrates grossly disorganized thinking, and may also experience delusions or auditory hallucinations
Community psychology	Community psychology is the study of how to use the principles of psychology to create communities of all sizes that promote mental health of their members.
Acquisition	Acquisition is the process of adapting to the environment, learning or becoming conditioned. In classical conditoning terms, it is the initial learning of the stimulus response link, which involves a

	neutral stimulus being associated with a unconditioned stimulus and becoming a conditioned stimulus.
Correlational research	Research that examines the relationship between two sets of variables to determine whether they are associated is called correlational research.
Role model	A person who serves as a positive example of desirable behavior is referred to as a role model.
Analogy	An analogy is a comparison between two different things, in order to highlight some form of similarity. Analogy is the cognitive process of transferring information from a particular subject to another particular subject.
Quantitative	A quantitative property is one that exists in a range of magnitudes, and can therefore be measured. Measurements of any particular quantitative property are expressed as as a specific quantity, referred to as a unit, multiplied by a number.
Motivation	In psychology, motivation is the driving force (desire) behind all actions of an organism.
Identity crisis	Erikson coinded the term identity crisis: "...a psychosocial state or condition of disorientation and role confusion occurring especially in adolescents as a result of conflicting internal and external experiences, pressures, and expectations and often producing acute anxiety."
Exposure therapy	An exposure therapy is any method of treating fears, including flooding and systematic desensitization, that involves exposing the client to the feared object or situation so that the process of extinction or habituation of the fear response can occur.
Couples therapy	Therapy with married or unmarried couples whose major problem is within their relationship is referred to as couples therapy.
Gestalt therapy	Gestalt therapy is a form of psychotherapy, based on the experiential ideal of "here and now," and relationships with others and the world. By focusing the individual on their self-awareness as part of present reality, new insights can be made into their behavior, and they can engage in self-healing.
Brief therapy	A primary approach of brief therapy is to open up the present to admit a wider context and more appropriate understandings (not necessarily at a conscious level), rather than formal analysis of historical causes.
Idiographic	An idiographic investigation studies the characteristics of an individual in depth.

Clinical psychology	Clinical psychology is involved in the diagnosis, assessment, and treatment of patients with mental or behavioral disorders, and conducts research in these various areas.
Rousseau	Rousseau rejected the idea of the blank slate. He believed that learning was a natural consequence of human existence. Further, he thought socialization unimportant in development. Because of his insistence that childhood was different than adulthood and his creation of stages of development, he is known as the father of developmental psychology.
Idealism	Idealism relates to direct knowledge of subjective mental ideas, or images. It is usually juxtaposed with realism in which the real is said to have absolute existence prior to and independent of our knowledge.
Pinel	Pinel is regarded as the father of modern psychiatry. He was a clinician believing that medical truth derived from clinical experience. While at Bicêtre, Pinel did away with bleeding, purging, and blistering in favor a therapy that involved close contact with and careful observation of patients.
Mental illness	Mental illness is the term formerly used to mean psychological disorder but less preferred because it implies that the causes of the disorder can be found in a medical disease process.
Antecedents	In behavior modification, events that typically precede the target response are called antecedents.
Dorothea Dix	Dorothea Dix drew on the most advanced 19th-century ideas about psychiatric treatment to successfully lobby almost every State legislature to create asylums for the insane. Unfortunately for her legacy, these state hospitals grew into enormous museums of madness that served as the deserving targets for later reformers' zeal.
Wisdom	Wisdom is the ability to make correct judgments and decisions. It is an intangible quality gained through experience. Whether or not something is wise is determined in a pragmatic sense by its popularity, how long it has been around, and its ability to predict against future events.
Galton	Galton was one of the first experimental psychologists, and the founder of the field of Differential Psychology, which concerns itself with individual differences rather than on common trends. He created the statistical methods correlation and regression.
Quantitative	A quantitative property is one that exists in a range of magnitudes, and can therefore be measured. Measurements of any particular quantitative property are expressed as as a specific quantity, referred to as a unit, multiplied by a number.
Reaction time	The amount of time required to respond to a stimulus is referred to as reaction time.
James McKeen Cattell	James McKeen Cattell was the first professor of psychology in the United States. His major contribution to psychology was the realization of the importance, and subsequent implementation, of quantitative methodologies and techniques. He coined the term "mental test" 1890.
Attention	Attention is the cognitive process of selectively concentrating on one thing while ignoring other things. Psychologists have labeled three types of attention: sustained attention, selective attention, and divided attention.
Wundt	Wundt, considered the father of experimental psychology, created the first laboratory in psychology in 1879. His methodology was based on introspection and his body of work founded the school of thought called Voluntarism.
Psychiatrist	A psychiatrist is a physician who specializes in the diagnosis and treatment of psychological disorders.
Kraepelin	Kraepelin postulated that there is a specific brain or other biological pathology underlying

	each of the major psychiatric disorders. Just as his laboratory discovered the pathologic basis of what is now known as Alzheimers disease, Kraepelin was confident that it would someday be possible to identify the pathologic basis of each of the major psychiatric disorders.
Exogenous	Exogenous refers to an action or object coming from outside a system.
Scheme	According to Piaget, a hypothetical mental structure that permits the classification and organization of new information is called a scheme.
Psychopathology	Psychopathology refers to the field concerned with the nature and development of mental disorders.
Heuristic	A heuristic is a simple, efficient rule of thumb proposed to explain how people make decisions, come to judgments and solve problems, typically when facing complex problems or incomplete information. These rules work well under most circumstances, but in certain cases lead to systematic cognitive biases.
Psychological testing	Psychological testing is a field characterized by the use of small samples of behavior in order to infer larger generalizations about a given individual. The technical term for psychological testing is psychometrics.
Alfred Binet	Alfred Binet published the first modern intelligence test, the Binet-Simon intelligence scale, in 1905. Binet stressed that the core of intelligence consists of complex cognitive processes, such as memory, imagery, comprehension, and judgment; and, that these developed over time in the individual.
Norms	In testing, standards of test performance that permit the comparison of one person's score on the test to the scores of others who have taken the same test are referred to as norms.
Individual differences	Individual differences psychology studies the ways in which individual people differ in their behavior. This is distinguished from other aspects of psychology in that although psychology is ostensibly a study of individuals, modern psychologists invariably study groups.
Theodore Simon	Theodore Simon co-created the Stanford-Binet Intelligence Scale test with Alfred Binet.
Thorndike	Thorndike worked in animal behavior and the learning process leading to the theory of connectionism. Among his most famous contributions were his research on cats escaping from puzzle boxes, and his formulation of the Law of Effect.
Personality	Personality refers to the pattern of enduring characteristics that differentiates a person, the patterns of behaviors that make each individual unique.
Goddard	Goddard is known especially for his 1912 work, The Kallikak Family: A Study in the Heredity of Feeble-Mindedness and for being the first to translate the Binet intelligence test into English in 1908.
Jung	Jung was in some aspects a response to Sigmund Freud's psychoanalysis. He proposed and developed the concepts of the extroverted and introverted personality, archetypes, and the collective unconscious. His work has been influential in psychiatry and in the study of religion, literature, and related fields.
Free association	In psychoanalysis, the uncensored uttering of all thoughts that come to mind is called free association.
Charles Spearman	Charles Spearman is known for his work in statistics, as a pioneer of factor analysis, and for his rank correlation coefficient. He also did seminal work on models for human intelligence, including discovering that disparate cognitive test scores reflect a single general factor and coining the term g factor.
American	The American Psychological Association is a professional organization representing psychology

Psychological Association in the US. The mission statement is to "advance psychology as a science and profession and as a means of promoting health, education , and human welfare".

Abnormal behavior An action, thought, or feeling that is harmful to the person or to others is called abnormal behavior.

Questionnaire A self-report method of data collection or clinical assessment method in which the individual being studied checks off items on a printed list, answers multiple-choice questions, or writes out answers to essay questions aimed at producing a selfdescription is called questionnaire.

Clinician A health professional authorized to provide services to people suffering from one or more pathologies is a clinician.

Intelligence quotient An intelligence quotient is a score derived from a set of standardized tests that were developed with the purpose of measuring a person's cognitive abilities ("intelligence") in relation to their age group.

Factor analysis Factor analysis is a statistical technique that originated in psychometrics. The objective is to explain the most of the variability among a number of observable random variables in terms of a smaller number of unobservable random variables called factors.

Thurstone Thurstone was a pioneer in the field of psychometrics. His work in factor analysis led him to formulate a model of intelligence center around "Primary Mental Abilities", which were independent group factors of intelligence that different individuals possessed in varying degrees.

David Wechsler David Wechsler developed two well-known intelligence scales, namely the Wechsler Adult Intelligence Scale and the Wechsler Intelligence Scale for Children. He held the view that human intelligence is not a single thing, but a mixture of many distinct -- and separately measurable -- human capabilities.

Wechsler Wechsler is best known for his intelligence tests. The Wechsler Adult Intelligence Scale (WAIS) was developed first in 1939 and then called the Wechsler-Bellevue Intelligence Test. From these he derived the Wechsler Intelligence Scale for Children (WISC) in 1949 and the Wechsler Preschool and Primary Scale of Intelligence (WPPSI) in 1967. Wechsler originally created these tests to find out more about his patients at the Bellevue clinic and he found the then-current Binet IQ test unsatisfactory.

Emotion An emotion is a mental states that arise spontaneously, rather than through conscious effort. They are often accompanied by physiological changes.

Pressey In the early 1920s Pressey developed a machine to provide drill and practice items to students. The teaching machine that Pressey developed resembled a typewriter carriage with a window that revealed a question having four answers.

Allport Allport was a trait theorist. Those traits he believed to predominate a person's personality were called central traits. Traits such that one could be indentifed by the trait, were referred to as cardinal traits. Central traits and cardinal traits are influenced by environmental factors.

Rorschach The Rorschach inkblot test is a method of psychological evaluation. It is a projective test associated with the Freudian school of thought. Psychologists use this test to try to probe the unconscious minds of their patients.

Stimulus A change in an environmental condition that elicits a response is a stimulus.

Beck Beck was initially trained as a psychoanalyst and conducted research on the psychoanalytic treatment of depression. With out the strong ability to collect data to this end, he began exploring cognitive approaches to treatment and originated cognitive behavior therapy.

Henry Murray	Henry Murray believed that personality could be better understood by investigating the unconscious mind. He is most famous for the development of the Thematic Apperception Test (TAT), a widely used projective measure of personality.
Apperception	A newly experienced sensation is related to past experiences to form an understood situation. For Wundt, consciousness is composed of two "stages:" There is a large capacity working memory called the Blickfeld and the narrower consciousness called Apperception, or selective attention.
Thematic Apperception Test	The Thematic Apperception Test uses a standard series of provocative yet ambiguous pictures about which the subject must tell a story. Each story is carefully analyzed to uncover underlying needs, attitudes, and patterns of reaction.
Projective test	A projective test is a personality test designed to let a person respond to ambiguous stimuli, presumably revealing hidden emotions and internal conflicts. This is different from an "objective test" in which responses are analyzed according to a universal standard rather than an individual psychiatrist's judgement.
Intelligence test	An intelligence test is a standardized means of assessing a person's current mental ability, for example, the Stanford-Binet test and the Wechsler Adult Intelligence Scale.
Minnesota Multiphasic Personality Inventory	The Minnesota Multiphasic Personality Inventory is the most frequently used test in the mental health fields. This assessment or test helps identify personal, social, and behavioral problems in psychiatric patients. This test helps provide relevant information to aid in problem identification, diagnosis, and treatment planning for the patient.
Personality inventory	A self-report questionnaire by which an examinee indicates whether statements assessing habitual tendencies apply to him or her is referred to as a personality inventory.
Cronbach	Cronbach is most famous for the development of Cronbach's alpha, a method for determining the reliability of educational and psychological tests. His work on test reliability reached an acme with the creation of generalizability theory, a statistical model for identifying and quantifying the sources of measurement error.
Attitude	An enduring mental representation of a person, place, or thing that evokes an emotional response and related behavior is called attitude.
Wechsler Adult Intelligence Scale	Wechsler adult intelligence scale is an individual intelligence test for adults that yields separate verbal and performance IQ scores as well as an overall IQ score.
Wechsler adult Intelligence	Wechsler adult Intelligence Scale is a revision of the Wechsler-Bellevue test (1939), standardized for use with adults over the age of 16.
Personality test	A personality test aims to describe aspects of a person's character that remain stable across situations.
Terman	Terman revised the Stanford-Binet Intelligence Scale in 1916, commonly used to measure intelligence (or I.Q.) in the United States. William Stern's suggestion that mental age/chronological age times 100 (to get rid of the decimal) be made the "intelligence quotient" or I.Q. This apparent mathematization of the measurement gave it an air of scientific accuracy and detachment which contributed greatly to its acceptance among educators and the broad public.
Test battery	A group of tests and interviews given to the same individual is a test battery.
Neuropsychol-gical test	A neuropsychological test use specifically designed tasks used to measure a psychological function known to be linked to a particular brain structure or pathway. They usually involve the systematic administration of clearly defined procedures in a formal environment.

Managed health care	A term that refers to the industrialization of health care, whereby large organizations in the private sector control the delivery of services is called managed health care.
Psychological test	Psychological test refers to a standardized measure of a sample of a person's behavior.
Psychodiagnosis	Psychodiagnosis is an attempt to describe, assess, and systematically draw inferences about an individual's psychological disorder.
Clinical psychologist	A psychologist, usually with a Ph.D, whose training is in the diagnosis, treatment, or research of psychological and behavioral disorders is a clinical psychologist.
Idiographic	An idiographic investigation studies the characteristics of an individual in depth.
Psychodynamic	Most psychodynamic approaches are centered around the idea of a maladapted function developed early in life (usually childhood) which are at least in part unconscious. This maladapted function (a.k.a. defense mechanism) does not do well in place of a normal/healthy one.
Behaviorism	The school of psychology that defines psychology as the study of observable behavior and studies relationships between stimuli and responses is called behaviorism. Behaviorism relied heavily on animal research and stated the same principles governed the behavior of both nonhumans and humans.
Radical behaviorism	Skinner defined behavior to include everything that an organism does, including thinking, feeling and speaking and argued that these phenomena were valid subject matters of psychology. The term Radical Behaviorism refers to "everything an organism does is a behavior."
Personality trait	According to the Diagnostic and Statistical Manual of the American Psychiatric Association, a personality trait is a "prominent aspect of personality that is exhibited in a wide range of important social and personal contexts. ...".
Overt behavior	An action or response that is directly observable and measurable is an overt behavior.
Trait	An enduring personality characteristic that tends to lead to certain behaviors is called a trait. The term trait also means a genetically inherited feature of an organism.
Mischel	Mischel is known for his cognitive social learning model of personality that focuses on the specific cognitive variables that mediate the manner in which new experiences affect the individual.
Behavioral assessment	Direct measures of an individual's behavior used to describe characteristics indicative of personality are called behavioral assessment.
Mental disorder	Mental disorder refers to a disturbance in a person's emotions, drives, thought processes, or behavior that involves serious and relatively prolonged distress and/or impairment in ability to function, is not simply a normal response to some event or set of events in the person's environment.
Resurgence	Resurgence refers to the reappearance during extinction, of a previously reinforced behavior.
Empirical	Empirical means the use of working hypotheses which are capable of being disproved using observation or experiment.
Millon Clinical Multiaxial Inventory	The Millon Clinical Multiaxial Inventory is a self-report assessment of personality disorders and clinical syndromes. This is sometimes used as an adjunct instrument in comprehensive neuropsychological assessment.
Personality disorder	A mental disorder characterized by a set of inflexible, maladaptive personality traits that keep a person from functioning properly in society is referred to as a personality disorder.
Clinical	A clinical assessment is a systematic evaluation and measurement of psychological,

assessment	biological, and social factors in a person presenting with a possible psychological disorder.
Brain	The brain controls and coordinates most movement, behavior and homeostatic body functions such as heartbeat, blood pressure, fluid balance and body temperature. Functions of the brain are responsible for cognition, emotion, memory, motor learning and other sorts of learning. The brain is primarily made up of two types of cells: glia and neurons.
Neuropsychology	Neuropsychology is a branch of psychology that aims to understand how the structure and function of the brain relates to specific psychological processes.
Hysteria	Hysteria is a diagnostic label applied to a state of mind, one of unmanageable fear or emotional excesses. The fear is often centered on a body part, most often on an imagined problem with that body part.
Sigmund Freud	Sigmund Freud was the founder of the psychoanalytic school, based on his theory that unconscious motives control much behavior, that particular kinds of unconscious thoughts and memories are the source of neurosis, and that neurosis could be treated through bringing these unconscious thoughts and memories to consciousness in psychoanalytic treatment.
Breuer	Breuer is perhaps best known for his work with Anna O. – a woman suffering with symptoms of paralysis, anaesthesias, and disturbances of vision and speech. The discussions of Anna O. between Freud and Breuer were documented in their Studies in Hysteria and became a formative basis of Freudian theory and psychoanalytic practice.
Psychotherapy	Psychotherapy is a set of techniques based on psychological principles intended to improve mental health, emotional or behavioral issues.
Charcot	Charcot took an interest in the malady then called hysteria. It seemed to be a mental disorder with physical manifestations, of immediate interest to a neurologist. He believed that hysteria was the result of a weak neurological system which was hereditary.
Depression	In everyday language depression refers to any downturn in mood, which may be relatively transitory and perhaps due to something trivial. This is differentiated from Clinical depression which is marked by symptoms that last two weeks or more and are so severe that they interfere with daily living.
Neurologist	A physician who studies the nervous system, especially its structure, functions, and abnormalities is referred to as neurologist.
The Interpretation of Dreams	The Interpretation of Dreams is a book by Sigmund Freud. The book introduces the Id, the Ego, and the Superego, and describes Freud's theory of the unconscious with respect to Dream interpretation. Widely considered to be his most important contribution to Psychology.
Oedipus complex	The Oedipus complex is a concept developed by Sigmund Freud to explain the maturation of the infant boy through identification with the father and desire for the mother.
Ego	In Freud's view the Ego serves to balance our primitive needs and our moral beliefs and taboos. Relying on experience, a healthy Ego provides the ability to adapt to reality and interact with the outside world.
Adler	Adler argued that human personality could be explained teleologically, separate strands dominated by the guiding purpose of the individual's unconscious self ideal to convert feelings of inferiority to superiority (or rather completeness). The desires of the self ideal were countered by social and ethical demands.
Ernest Jones	Ernest Jones was arguably the best-known follower of Freud. His writings on the subject of psychoanalysis prompted him to launch The International Journal of Psychoanalysis in 1920.
Otto Rank	Otto Rank extended psychoanalytic theory to the study of legend, myth, art, and other works of creativity. He favored a more egalitarian relationship with patients and is sometimes

	considered the forerunner of client-centered therapy.
Launching	The process in which youths move into adulthood and exit their family of origin is called launching. It can be a time to formulate life goals, to develop an identity, and to become more independent before joining with another person to form a new family.
Psychoanalysis	Psychoanalysis refers to the school of psychology that emphasizes the importance of unconscious motives and conflicts as determinants of human behavior. It was Freud's method of exploring human personality.
Psychoanalyst	A psychoanalyst is a specially trained therapist who attempts to treat the individual by uncovering and revealing to the individual otherwise subconscious factors that are contributing to some undesirable behavor.
Psychoanalytic	Freud's theory that unconscious forces act as determinants of personality is called psychoanalytic theory. The theory is a developmental theory characterized by critical stages of development.
Play therapy	Play therapy is often used to help the diagnostician to try to determine the cause of disturbed behavior in a child. Treatment therapists then used a type of systematic desensitization or relearning therapy to change the disturbing behavior, either systematically or in less formal social settings.
Anxiety	Anxiety is a complex combination of the feeling of fear, apprehension and worry often accompanied by physical sensations such as palpitations, chest pain and/or shortness of breath.
Anna Freud	Anna Freud was a pioneer of child psychoanalysis. She popularized the notion that adolescence is a period that includes rapid mood fluctuation with enormous uncertainty about self.
Mary Cover Jones	Mary Cover Jones stands out as a pioneer of behavior therapy. Her study of unconditioning a fear of rabbits in a three-year-old named Peter is her most often cited work.
Conditioning	Conditioning describes the process by which behaviors can be learned or modified through interaction with the environment.
Watson	Watson, the father of behaviorism, developed the term "Behaviorism" as a name for his proposal to revolutionize the study of human psychology in order to put it on a firm experimental footing.
Family therapy	Family therapy is a branch of psychotherapy that treats family problems. Family therapists consider the family as a system of interacting members; as such, the problems in the family are seen to arise as an emergent property of the interactions in the system, rather than ascribed exclusively to the "faults" or psychological problems of individual members.
Reflex	A simple, involuntary response to a stimulus is referred to as reflex. Reflex actions originate at the spinal cord rather than the brain.
Conditioned reflex	The conditioned reflex was Pavlov's term for the conditioned response which is a an acquired response that is under the control of (conditional on the occurrence of) a stimulus
Desensitization	Desensitization refers to the type of sensory or behavioral adaptation in which we become less sensitive to constant stimuli.
Behavioral therapy	The treatment of a mental disorder through the application of basic principles of conditioning and learning is called behavioral therapy.
Skinner	Skinner conducted research on shaping behavior through positive and negative reinforcement, and demonstrated operant conditioning, a technique which he developed in contrast with classical conditioning.

Modeling	A type of behavior learned through observation of others demonstrating the same behavior is modeling.
Bandura	Bandura is best known for his work on social learning theory or Social Cognitivism. His famous Bobo doll experiment illustrated that people learn from observing others.
Behavior therapy	Behavior therapy refers to the systematic application of the principles of learning to direct modification of a client's problem behaviors.
Anxiety disorder	Anxiety disorder is a blanket term covering several different forms of abnormal anxiety, fear, phobia and nervous condition, that come on suddenly and prevent pursuing normal daily routines.
Health psychology	The field of psychology that studies the relationships between psychological factors and the prevention and treatment of physical illness is called health psychology.
Asylums	Asylums are hospitals specializing in the treatment of persons with mental illness. Psychiatric wards differ only in that they are a unit of a larger hospital.
Wolpe	Wolpe is best known for applying classical conditioning principles to the treatment of phobias, called systematic desensitization. Any "neutral" stimulus, simple or complex that happens to make an impact on an individual at about the time that a fear reaction is evoked acquires the ability to evoke fear subsequently. An acquired CS-CR relationship should be extinguishable.
Systematic desensitization	Systematic desensitization refers to Wolpe's behavioral fear-reduction technique in which a hierarchy of fear-evoking stimuli are presented while the person remains relaxed. The fear-evoking stimuli thereby become associated with muscle relaxation.
Community psychology	Community psychology is the study of how to use the principles of psychology to create communities of all sizes that promote mental health of their members.
Affect	A subjective feeling or emotional tone often accompanied by bodily expressions noticeable to others is called affect.
William James	Functionalism as a psychology developed out of Pragmatism as a philosophy: To find the meaning of an idea, you have to look at its consequences. This led William James and his students towards an emphasis on cause and effect, prediction and control, and observation of environment and behavior, over the careful introspection of the Structuralists.
Pavlov	Pavlov first described the phenomenon now known as classical conditioning in experiments with dogs.
Classical conditioning	Classical conditioning is a simple form of learning in which an organism comes to associate or anticipate events. A neutral stimulus comes to evoke the response usually evoked by a natural or unconditioned stimulus by being paired repeatedly with the unconditioned stimulus.
Validity	The extent to which a test measures what it is intended to measure is called validity.
Infancy	The developmental period that extends from birth to 18 or 24 months is called infancy.
Gestalt psychology	According to Gestalt psychology, people naturally organize their perceptions according to certain patterns. The tendency is to organize perceptions into wholes and to integrate separate stimuli into meaningful patterns.
Perception	Perception is the process of acquiring, interpreting, selecting, and organizing sensory information.
Wechsler Scales	The Wechsler Scales are two well-known intelligence scales, namely the Wechsler Adult Intelligence Scale and the Wechsler Intelligence Scale for Children.
Reliability	Reliability means the extent to which a test produces a consistent , reproducible score .

Carl Rogers
Carl Rogers was instrumental in the development of non-directive psychotherapy, also known as "client-centered" psychotherapy. Rogers' basic tenets were unconditional positive regard, genuineness, and empathic understanding, with each demonstrated by the counselor.

Social learning
Social learning is learning that occurs as a function of observing, retaining and replicating behavior observed in others. Although social learning can occur at any stage in life, it is thought to be particularly important during childhood, particularly as authority becomes important.

Learning
Learning is a relatively permanent change in behavior that results from experience. Thus, to attribute a behavioral change to learning, the change must be relatively permanent and must result from experience.

Rotter
Rotter focused on the application of social learning theory (SLT) to clinical psychology. She introduced the ideas of learning from generalized expectancies of reinforcement and internal/ external locus of control (self-initiated change versus change influenced by others). According to Rotter, health outcomes could be improved by the development of a sense of personal control over one's life.

Social learning theory
Social learning theory explains the process of gender typing in terms of observation, imitation, and role playing .

Insight
Insight refers to a sudden awareness of the relationships among various elements that had previously appeared to be independent of one another.

Major depression
Major depression is characterized by a severely depressed mood that persists for at least two weeks. Episodes of depression may start suddenly or slowly and can occur several times through a person's life. The disorder may be categorized as "single episode" or "recurrent" depending on whether previous episodes have been experienced before.

Schizophrenia
Schizophrenia is characterized by persistent defects in the perception or expression of reality. A person suffering from untreated schizophrenia typically demonstrates grossly disorganized thinking, and may also experience delusions or auditory hallucinations

Syndrome
The term syndrome is the association of several clinically recognizable features, signs, symptoms, phenomena or characteristics which often occur together, so that the presence of one feature indicates the presence of the others.

Antisocial personality
A disorder in which individuals tend to display no regard for the moral and ethical rules of society or the rights of others is called antisocial personality disorder.

Predisposition
Predisposition refers to an inclination or diathesis to respond in a certain way, either inborn or acquired. In abnormal psychology, it is a factor that lowers the ability to withstand stress and inclines the individual toward pathology.

Sexual abuse
Sexual abuse is a term used to describe non- consentual sexual relations between two or more parties which are considered criminally and/or morally offensive.

Genetics
Genetics is the science of genes, heredity, and the variation of organisms.

Behavioral genetics
Behavioral genetics is the field of biology that studies the role of genetics in behavior.

Witmer
Witmer first described and coined the terms clinical psychology and psychological clinic. In the beginning of clinical psychology, pioneers such as Witmer saw the benefit of a collaboration between mental health and medical health care provision.

Abnormal psychology
The scientific study whose objectives are to describe, explain, predict, and control behaviors that are considered strange or unusual is referred to as abnormal psychology.

Mental
Mental retardation refers to having significantly below-average intellectual functioning and

retardation	limitations in at least two areas of adaptive functioning. Many categorize retardation as mild, moderate, severe, or profound.
Educational psychology	Educational psychology is the study of how children and adults learn, the effectiveness of various educational strategies and tactics, and how schools function as organizations.
Research method	The scope of the research method is to produce some new knowledge. This, in principle, can take three main forms: Exploratory research; Constructive research; and Empirical research.
Trauma	Trauma refers to a severe physical injury or wound to the body caused by an external force, or a psychological shock having a lasting effect on mental life.
Reinforcement	In operant conditioning, reinforcement is any change in an environment that (a) occurs after the behavior, (b) seems to make that behavior re-occur more often in the future and (c) that reoccurence of behavior must be the result of the change.
Reinforcement contingencies	The circumstances or rules that determine whether responses lead to the presentation of reinforcers are referred to as reinforcement contingencies. Skinner defined culture as a set of reinforcement contingencies.
Sexual dysfunction	Sexual dysfunction is difficulty during any stage of the sexual act (which includes desire, arousal, orgasm, and resolution) that prevents the individual or couple from enjoying sexual activity.
Assertiveness	Assertiveness basically means the ability to express your thoughts and feelings in a way that clearly states your needs and keeps the lines of communication open with the other.
Alcoholism	A disorder that involves long-term, repeated, uncontrolled, compulsive, and excessive use of alcoholic beverages and that impairs the drinker's health and work and social relationships is called alcoholism.
Obesity	The state of being more than 20 percent above the average weight for a person of one's height is called obesity.
Cognition	The intellectual processes through which information is obtained, transformed, stored, retrieved, and otherwise used is cognition.
Society	The social sciences use the term society to mean a group of people that form a semi-closed (or semi-open) social system, in which most interactions are with other individuals belonging to the group.
Brief therapy	A primary approach of brief therapy is to open up the present to admit a wider context and more appropriate understandings (not necessarily at a conscious level), rather than formal analysis of historical causes.
Presenting problem	The presenting problem is the original complaint reported by the client to the therapist. The actual treated problem may sometimes be a modification derived from the presenting problem or entirely different..
Nomothetic	Nomothetic measures are contrasted to ipsative or idiothetic measures, where nomothetic measures are measures that can be taken directly by an outside observer, such as weight or how many times a particular behavior occurs, and ipsative measures are self-reports such as a rank-ordered list of preferences.
Adolescence	The period of life bounded by puberty and the assumption of adult responsibilities is adolescence.
Maladaptive	In psychology, a behavior or trait is adaptive when it helps an individual adjust and function well within their social environment. A maladaptive behavior or trait is counterproductive to the individual.

Clinical psychology — Clinical psychology is involved in the diagnosis, assessment, and treatment of patients with mental or behavioral disorders, and conducts research in these various areas.

Psychotherapy — Psychotherapy is a set of techniques based on psychological principles intended to improve mental health, emotional or behavioral issues.

Conditioning — Conditioning describes the process by which behaviors can be learned or modified through interaction with the environment.

Learning — Learning is a relatively permanent change in behavior that results from experience. Thus, to attribute a behavioral change to learning, the change must be relatively permanent and must result from experience.

Variance — The degree to which scores differ among individuals in a distribution of scores is the variance.

Theories — Theories are logically self-consistent models or frameworks describing the behavior of a certain natural or social phenomenon. They are broad explanations and predictions concerning phenomena of interest.

Physiological psychology — Physiological psychology refers to the study of the physiological mechanisms, in the brain and elsewhere, that mediate behavior and psychological experiences.

Analysis of variance — Analysis of variance is an inferential statistical technique used to compare differences between two or more groups with the purpose of making a decision whether the groups come from the same population or not.

Clinician — A health professional authorized to provide services to people suffering from one or more pathologies is a clinician.

Empiricism — Empiricism is generally regarded as being at the heart of the modern scientific method, that our theories should be based on our observations of the world rather than on intuition, or deductive logic.

Quantitative — A quantitative property is one that exists in a range of magnitudes, and can therefore be measured. Measurements of any particular quantitative property are expressed as as a specific quantity, referred to as a unit, multiplied by a number.

Clinical psychologist — A psychologist, usually with a Ph.D, whose training is in the diagnosis, treatment, or research of psychological and behavioral disorders is a clinical psychologist.

Inference — Inference is the act or process of drawing a conclusion based solely on what one already knows.

Role model — A person who serves as a positive example of desirable behavior is referred to as a role model.

Clinical study — An intensive investigation of a single person, especially one suffering from some injury or disease is referred to as a clinical study.

Empirical — Empirical means the use of working hypotheses which are capable of being disproved using observation or experiment.

Society — The social sciences use the term society to mean a group of people that form a semi-closed (or semi-open) social system, in which most interactions are with other individuals belonging to the group.

Fisher — Fisher was a eugenicist, evolutionary biologist, geneticist and statistician. He has been described as "The greatest of Darwin's successors", and a genius who almost single-handedly created the foundations for modern statistical science inventing the techniques of maximum likelihood and analysis of variance.

Psychopathology	Psychopathology refers to the field concerned with the nature and development of mental disorders.
Etiology	Etiology is the study of causation. The term is used in philosophy, physics and biology in reference to the causes of various phenomena. It is generally the study of why things occur, or even the reasons behind the way that things act.
Eating disorders	Psychological disorders characterized by distortion of the body image and gross disturbances in eating patterns are called eating disorders.
Population	Population refers to all members of a well-defined group of organisms, events, or things.
Depression	In everyday language depression refers to any downturn in mood, which may be relatively transitory and perhaps due to something trivial. This is differentiated from Clinical depression which is marked by symptoms that last two weeks or more and are so severe that they interfere with daily living.
Addiction	Addiction is an uncontrollable compulsion to repeat a behavior regardless of its consequences. Many drugs or behaviors can precipitate a pattern of conditions recognized as addiction, which include a craving for more of the drug or behavior, increased physiological tolerance to exposure, and withdrawal symptoms in the absence of the stimulus.
Juvenile delinquent	An adolescent who breaks the law or engages in behavior that is considered illegal is referred to as a juvenile delinquent.
Cognitive science	Cognitive Science is the scientific study of the mind and brain and how they give rise to behavior. The field is highly interdisciplinary and is closely related to several other areas, including psychology, artificial intelligence, linguistics and psycholinguistics, philosophy, neuroscience, logic, robotics, anthropology and biology.
Neuroscience	A field that combines the work of psychologists, biologists, biochemists, medical researchers, and others in the study of the structure and function of the nervous system is neuroscience.
Psychiatrist	A psychiatrist is a physician who specializes in the diagnosis and treatment of psychological disorders.
American Psychological Association	The American Psychological Association is a professional organization representing psychology in the US. The mission statement is to "advance psychology as a science and profession and as a means of promoting health, education , and human welfare".
Threshold	In general, a threshold is a fixed location or value where an abrupt change is observed. In the sensory modalities, it is the minimum amount of stimulus energy necessary to elicit a sensory response.
Moral character	Moral character or character is an abstract evaluation of a person's moral and mental qualities. Such an evaluation is subjective — one person may evaluate someone's character on the basis of their virtue, another may consider their fortitude, courage, loyalty, honesty, or piety.
Health psychology	The field of psychology that studies the relationships between psychological factors and the prevention and treatment of physical illness is called health psychology.
Neuropsychology	Neuropsychology is a branch of psychology that aims to understand how the structure and function of the brain relates to specific psychological processes.
Psychoanalysis	Psychoanalysis refers to the school of psychology that emphasizes the importance of unconscious motives and conflicts as determinants of human behavior. It was Freud's method of exploring human personality.
Behavioral	Behavioral psychology is an approach to psychology based on the proposition that behavior can

psychology	be researched scientifically without recourse to inner mental states. It is a form of materialism, denying any independent significance for the mind.
Counseling psychology	Counseling psychology is unique in its attention both to normal developmental issues and to problems associated with physical, emotional, and mental disorders.
Forensic psychology	Psychological research and theory that deals with the effects of cognitive, affective, and behavioral factors on legal proceedings and the law is a forensic psychology.
Managed health care	A term that refers to the industrialization of health care, whereby large organizations in the private sector control the delivery of services is called managed health care.
Applied research	Applied research is done to solve specific, practical questions; its primary aim is not to gain knowledge for its own sake. It can be exploratory but often it is descriptive. It is almost always done on the basis of basic research.
Paradigm shift	A paradigm shift is the process and result of a change in basic assumptions within the ruling theory of science.
Paradigm	Paradigm refers to the set of practices that defines a scientific discipline during a particular period of time. It provides a framework from which to conduct research, it ensures that a certain range of phenomena, those on which the paradigm focuses, are explored thoroughly. Itmay also blind scientists to other, perhaps more fruitful, ways of dealing with their subject matter.
Alcoholic	An alcoholic is dependent on alcohol as characterized by craving, loss of control, physical dependence and withdrawal symptoms, and tolerance.
Alcoholics Anonymous	The primary purpose of Alcoholics Anonymous membership is to stay sober and help others do the same. It. formed the original twelve-step program and has been the source and model for all similar recovery groups.
Paraprofessional	A paraprofessional is an individual lacking a doctoral degree but trained to perform certain functions usually reserved for clinicians.
Autonomy	Autonomy is the condition of something that does not depend on anything else.
Incentive	An incentive is what is expected once a behavior is performed. An incentive acts as a reinforcer.
Graham	Graham has conducted a number of studies that reveal stronger socioeconomic-status influences rather than ethnic influences in achievement.
Schizophrenia	Schizophrenia is characterized by persistent defects in the perception or expression of reality. A person suffering from untreated schizophrenia typically demonstrates grossly disorganized thinking, and may also experience delusions or auditory hallucinations
Affect	A subjective feeling or emotional tone often accompanied by bodily expressions noticeable to others is called affect.
Psychopharma-ology	Psychopharmacology refers to the study of the effects of drugs on the mind and on behavior; also known as medication and drug therapy.
Cocaine	Cocaine is a crystalline tropane alkaloid that is obtained from the leaves of the coca plant. It is a stimulant of the central nervous system and an appetite suppressant, creating what has been described as a euphoric sense of happiness and increased energy.
Survey	A method of scientific investigation in which a large sample of people answer questions about their attitudes or behavior is referred to as a survey.
Drug interaction	A combined effect of two drugs that exceeds the addition of one drug's effects to the other is a drug interaction.

Stereotype	A stereotype is considered to be a group concept, held by one social group about another.They are often used in a negative or prejudicial sense and are frequently used to justify certain discriminatory behaviors. This allows powerful social groups to legitimize and protect their dominant position
Cultural diversity	Cultural diversity is the variety of human societies or cultures in a specific region, or in the world as a whole.
Gender difference	A gender difference is a disparity between genders involving quality or quantity. Though some gender differences are controversial, they are not to be confused with sexist stereotypes.
Counseling psychologist	A doctoral level mental health professional whose training is similar to that of a clinical psychologist, though usually with less emphasis on research and serious psychopathology is referred to as a counseling psychologist.
Sexual orientation	Sexual orientation refers to the sex or gender of people who are the focus of a person's amorous or erotic desires, fantasies, and spontaneous feelings, the gender(s) toward which one is primarily "oriented".
Socioeconomic	Socioeconomic pertains to the study of the social and economic impacts of any product or service offering, market intervention or other activity on an economy as a whole and on the companies, organization and individuals who are its main economic actors.
Socioeconomic Status	A family's socioeconomic status is based on family income, parental education level, parental occupation, and social status in the community. Those with high status often have more success in preparing their children for school because they have access to a wide range of resources.
Child abuse	Child abuse is the physical or psychological maltreatment of a child.
Sexual harassment	Deliberate or repeated verbal comments, gestures, or physical contact of a sexual nature that is unwanted by the recipient is called sexual harassment.
Research method	The scope of the research method is to produce some new knowledge. This, in principle, can take three main forms: Exploratory research; Constructive research; and Empirical research.

Clinical psychologist	A psychologist, usually with a Ph.D, whose training is in the diagnosis, treatment, or research of psychological and behavioral disorders is a clinical psychologist.
Research method	The scope of the research method is to produce some new knowledge. This, in principle, can take three main forms: Exploratory research; Constructive research; and Empirical research.
Clinical psychology	Clinical psychology is involved in the diagnosis, assessment, and treatment of patients with mental or behavioral disorders, and conducts research in these various areas.
Suicide	Suicide behavior is rare in childhood but escalates in adolescence. The suicide rate increases in a linear fashion from adolescence through late adulthood.
Insight	Insight refers to a sudden awareness of the relationships among various elements that had previously appeared to be independent of one another.
Projective test	A projective test is a personality test designed to let a person respond to ambiguous stimuli, presumably revealing hidden emotions and internal conflicts. This is different from an "objective test" in which responses are analyzed according to a universal standard rather than an individual psychiatrist's judgement.
Attitude	An enduring mental representation of a person, place, or thing that evokes an emotional response and related behavior is called attitude.
Clinician	A health professional authorized to provide services to people suffering from one or more pathologies is a clinician.
Theories	Theories are logically self-consistent models or frameworks describing the behavior of a certain natural or social phenomenon. They are broad explanations and predictions concerning phenomena of interest.
Parsimony	In science, parsimony is preference for the least complicated explanation for an observation. This is generally regarded as good when judging hypotheses. Occam's Razor also states the "principle of parsimony".
Autonomy	Autonomy is the condition of something that does not depend on anything else.
Personality	Personality refers to the pattern of enduring characteristics that differentiates a person, the patterns of behaviors that make each individual unique.
Hypothesis	A specific statement about behavior or mental processes that is testable through research is a hypothesis.
Depression	In everyday language depression refers to any downturn in mood, which may be relatively transitory and perhaps due to something trivial. This is differentiated from Clinical depression which is marked by symptoms that last two weeks or more and are so severe that they interfere with daily living.
Beck	Beck was initially trained as a psychoanalyst and conducted research on the psychoanalytic treatment of depression. With out the strong ability to collect data to this end, he began exploring cognitive approaches to treatment and originated cognitive behavior therapy.
Case study	A carefully drawn biography that may be obtained through interviews, questionnaires, and psychological tests is called a case study.
Achievement test	A test designed to determine a person's level of knowledge in a given subject area is referred to as an achievement test.
Representative sample	Representative sample refers to a sample of participants selected from the larger population in such a way that important subgroups within the population are included in the sample in the same proportions as they are found in the larger population.
Naturalistic	Naturalistic observation is a method of observation that involves observing subjects in

observation	their natural habitats. Researchers take great care in avoiding making interferences with the behavior they are observing by using unobtrusive methods.
Construct	A generalized concept, such as anxiety or gravity, is a construct.
Problem solving	An attempt to find an appropriate way of attaining a goal when the goal is not readily available is called problem solving.
Specific phobia	A specific phobia is a generic term for anxiety disorders that amount to unreasonable or irrational fear or anxiety related with exposure to specific objects or situations. As a result, the affected persons tend to actively avoid these objects or situations.
Conditioning	Conditioning describes the process by which behaviors can be learned or modified through interaction with the environment.
Learning	Learning is a relatively permanent change in behavior that results from experience. Thus, to attribute a behavioral change to learning, the change must be relatively permanent and must result from experience.
Phobia	A persistent, irrational fear of an object, situation, or activity that the person feels compelled to avoid is referred to as a phobia.
Classical conditioning	Classical conditioning is a simple form of learning in which an organism comes to associate or anticipate events. A neutral stimulus comes to evoke the response usually evoked by a natural or unconditioned stimulus by being paired repeatedly with the unconditioned stimulus.
Little Albert	The Little Albert experiment was an experiment showing empirical evidence of classical conditioning in children. The actual experiment with Little Albert on conditioned fear involved exposing the child to a loud sound while being presented with a white rat.
Watson	Watson, the father of behaviorism, developed the term "Behaviorism" as a name for his proposal to revolutionize the study of human psychology in order to put it on a firm experimental footing.
Psychodynamic	Most psychodynamic approaches are centered around the idea of a maladapted function developed early in life (usually childhood) which are at least in part unconscious. This maladapted function (a.k.a. defense mechanism) does not do well in place of a normal/healthy one.
Trauma	Trauma refers to a severe physical injury or wound to the body caused by an external force, or a psychological shock having a lasting effect on mental life.
Anatomy	Anatomy is the branch of biology that deals with the structure and organization of living things. It can be divided into animal anatomy (zootomy) and plant anatomy (phytonomy). Major branches of anatomy include comparative anatomy, histology, and human anatomy.
Sanity	Sanity considered as a legal term denotes that an individual is of sound mind and therefore can bear legal responsibility for his or her actions.
Behavior modification	Behavior Modification is a technique of altering an individual's reactions to stimuli through positive reinforcement and the extinction of maladaptive behavior.
Allport	Allport was a trait theorist. Those traits he believed to predominate a person's personality were called central traits. Traits such that one could be indentifed by the trait, were referred to as cardinal traits. Central traits and cardinal traits are influenced by environmental factors.
Epidemiology	Epidemiology is the study of the distribution and determinants of disease and disorders in human populations, and the use of its knowledge to control health problems.Epidemiology is considered the cornerstone methodology in all of public health research, and is highly regarded in evidence-based clinical medicine for identifying risk factors for disease and determining optimal treatment approaches to clinical practice.

Population	Population refers to all members of a well-defined group of organisms, events, or things.
Epidemiological research	The study of the rate and distribution of mental disorders in a population is referred to as epidemiological research.
Correlation	A statistical technique for determining the degree of association between two or more variables is referred to as correlation.
Causation	Causation concerns the time order relationship between two or more objects such that if a specific antecendent condition occurs the same consequent must always follow.
Mental illness	Mental illness is the term formerly used to mean psychological disorder but less preferred because it implies that the causes of the disorder can be found in a medical disease process.
Socioeconomic	Socioeconomic pertains to the study of the social and economic impacts of any product or service offering, market intervention or other activity on an economy as a whole and on the companies, organization and individuals who are its main economic actors.
Schizophrenia	Schizophrenia is characterized by persistent defects in the perception or expression of reality. A person suffering from untreated schizophrenia typically demonstrates grossly disorganized thinking, and may also experience delusions or auditory hallucinations
Social skills	Social skills are skills used to interact and communicate with others to assist status in the social structure and other motivations.
Reinforcement	In operant conditioning, reinforcement is any change in an environment that (a) occurs after the behavior, (b) seems to make that behavior re-occur more often in the future and (c) that reoccurence of behavior must be the result of the change.
Empirical	Empirical means the use of working hypotheses which are capable of being disproved using observation or experiment.
Survey	A method of scientific investigation in which a large sample of people answer questions about their attitudes or behavior is referred to as a survey.
Mental disorder	Mental disorder refers to a disturbance in a person's emotions, drives, thought processes, or behavior that involves serious and relatively prolonged distress and/or impairment in ability to function, is not simply a normal response to some event or set of events in the person's environment.
Anxiety disorder	Anxiety disorder is a blanket term covering several different forms of abnormal anxiety, fear, phobia and nervous condition, that come on suddenly and prevent pursuing normal daily routines.
Anxiety	Anxiety is a complex combination of the feeling of fear, apprehension and worry often accompanied by physical sensations such as palpitations, chest pain and/or shortness of breath.
Antisocial personality	A disorder in which individuals tend to display no regard for the moral and ethical rules of society or the rights of others is called antisocial personality disorder.
Personality disorder	A mental disorder characterized by a set of inflexible, maladaptive personality traits that keep a person from functioning properly in society is referred to as a personality disorder.
Socioeconomic Status	A family's socioeconomic status is based on family income, parental education level, parental occupation, and social status in the community. Those with high status often have more success in preparing their children for school because they have access to a wide range of resources.
Correlational method	A research method used to establish the degree of relationship between two characteristics, events, or behaviors is called a correlational method.

Variable	A variable refers to a measurable factor, characteristic, or attribute of an individual or a system.
Correlation coefficient	Correlation coefficient refers to a number from +1.00 to -1.00 that expresses the direction and extent of the relationship between two variables. The closer to 1, the stronger the relationship. The sign, + or -, indicates the direction.
Mood disorder	A mood disorder is a condition where the prevailing emotional mood is distorted or inappropriate to the circumstances.
Agoraphobia	An irrational fear of open, crowded places is called agoraphobia. Many people suffering from agoraphobia, however, are not afraid of the open spaces themselves, but of situations often associated with these spaces, such as social gatherings.
Lifetime prevalence rate	Lifetime prevalence rate refers to the proportion of a sample that has ever had a specified disorder.
Comorbidity	Comorbidity refers to the presence of more than one mental disorder occurring in an individual at the same time.
Perfect negative relationship	A perfect negative relationship refers to a mathematical relationship in which the correlation between two measures is exactly -1.00.
Negative relationship	An inverse relationship, often called a negative relationship, occurs when increases in one variable are matched by decreases in another variable.
Scatterplot	A scatterplot or scatter graph is a graph used in statistics to visually display and compare two or more sets of related quantitative, or numerical, data by displaying only finitely many points, each having a coordinate on a horizontal and a vertical axis.
Factor analysis	Factor analysis is a statistical technique that originated in psychometrics. The objective is to explain the most of the variability among a number of observable random variables in terms of a smaller number of unobservable random variables called factors.
Positive relationship	Statistically, a positive relationship refers to a mathematical relationship in which increases in one measure are matched by increases in the other.
Altruism	Altruism is being helpful to other people with little or no interest in being rewarded for one's efforts. This is distinct from merely helping others.
Empathy	Empathy is the recognition and understanding of the states of mind, including beliefs, desires and particularly emotions of others without injecting your own.
Longitudinal approach	The Longitudinal approach is a research strategy in which the same individuals are studied over a period of time, usually several years or more.
Longitudinal design	A research design in which investigators observe one group of subjects repeatedly over a period of time is called a longitudinal design.
Longitudinal study	Longitudinal study is a type of developmental study in which the same group of participants is followed and measured for an extended period of time, often years.
Longitudinal research	Research that studies the same subjects over an extended period of time, usually several years or more, is called longitudinal research.
Experimental group	Experimental group refers to any group receiving a treatment effect in an experiment.
Control group	A group that does not receive the treatment effect in an experiment is referred to as the control group or sometimes as the comparison group.

Experimental hypothesis	The experimental hypothesis is what the investigator assumes will happen in a scientific investigation if certain conditions are met or particular variables are manipulated.
Independent variable	A condition in a scientific study that is manipulated (assigned different values by a researcher) so that the effects of the manipulation may be observed is called an independent variable.
Dependent variable	A measure of an assumed effect of an independent variable is called the dependent variable.
Internal validity	Internal validity is a term pertaining to scientific research that signifies the extent to which the conditions within a research design were conducive to drawing the conclusions the researcher was interested in drawing.
Validity	The extent to which a test measures what it is intended to measure is called validity.
Experimental manipulation	The change that an experimenter deliberately produces in a situation under study is called the experimental manipulation.
Random assignment	Assignment of participants to experimental and control groups by chance is called random assignment. Random assigment reduces the likelihood that the results are due to preexisiting systematic differences between the groups.
External validity	External validity is a term used in scientific research. It signifies the extent to which the results of a study can be applied to circumstances outside the specific setting in which the research was carried out. In other words, it addresses the question "Can this research be applied to 'the real world'?"
Generalization	In conditioning, the tendency for a conditioned response to be evoked by stimuli that are similar to the stimulus to which the response was conditioned is a generalization. The greater the similarity among the stimuli, the greater the probability of generalization.
Psychopathology	Psychopathology refers to the field concerned with the nature and development of mental disorders.
Analog study	An investigation that attempts to replicate or simulate, under controlled conditions, a situation that occurs in real life is an analog study.
Questionnaire	A self-report method of data collection or clinical assessment method in which the individual being studied checks off items on a printed list, answers multiple-choice questions, or writes out answers to essay questions aimed at producing a selfdescription is called questionnaire.
Laboratory setting	Research setting in which the behavior of interest does not naturally occur is called a laboratory setting.
Life span	Life span refers to the upper boundary of life, the maximum number of years an individual can live. The maximum life span of human beings is about 120 years of age. Females live an average of 6 years longer than males.
Personality trait	According to the Diagnostic and Statistical Manual of the American Psychiatric Association, a personality trait is a "prominent aspect of personality that is exhibited in a wide range of important social and personal contexts. ...".
Stimulus	A change in an environmental condition that elicits a response is a stimulus.
Affect	A subjective feeling or emotional tone often accompanied by bodily expressions noticeable to others is called affect.
Trait	An enduring personality characteristic that tends to lead to certain behaviors is called a trait. The term trait also means a genetically inherited feature of an organism.

Baseline	Measure of a particular behavior or process taken before the introduction of the independent variable or treatment is called the baseline.
Attention	Attention is the cognitive process of selectively concentrating on one thing while ignoring other things. Psychologists have labeled three types of attention: sustained attention, selective attention, and divided attention.
Major depression	Major depression is characterized by a severely depressed mood that persists for at least two weeks. Episodes of depression may start suddenly or slowly and can occur several times through a person's life. The disorder may be categorized as "single episode" or "recurrent" depending on whether previous episodes have been experienced before.
Generalized anxiety disorder	Generalized anxiety disorder is an anxiety disorder that is characterized by uncontrollable worry about everyday things. The frequency, intensity, and duration of the worry are disproportionate to the actual source of worry, and such worry often interferes with daily functioning.
Psychotherapy	Psychotherapy is a set of techniques based on psychological principles intended to improve mental health, emotional or behavioral issues.
Mixed design	Mixed design refer to an experimental situation that includes both within-subjects and between subjects components.
Beck Depression Inventory	The Beck Depression Inventory is a 21 question multiple choice survey that is one of the most widely used instruments for measuring depression severity.
Variance	The degree to which scores differ among individuals in a distribution of scores is the variance.
American Psychological Association	The American Psychological Association is a professional organization representing psychology in the US. The mission statement is to "advance psychology as a science and profession and as a means of promoting health, education , and human welfare".
Informed consent	The term used by psychologists to indicate that a person has agreed to participate in research after receiving information about the purposes of the study and the nature of the treatments is informed consent. Even with informed consent, subjects may withdraw from any experiment at any time.
Incentive	An incentive is what is expected once a behavior is performed. An incentive acts as a reinforcer.
Compensation	In personaility, compensation, according to Adler, is an effort to overcome imagined or real inferiorities by developing one's abilities.
Debriefing	Process of informing a participant after the experiment about the nature of the experiment, clarifying any misunderstanding, and answering any questions that the participant may have concerning the experiment is called debriefing.
Feedback	Feedback refers to information returned to a person about the effects a response has had.
Baseline period	In a within-subject experiment, a period of observation during which no attempt is made to modify the behavior under study is referred to as the baseline period.
Extraneous variables	Variables that are not directly related to the hypothesis under study and that the experimenter does not actively attempt to control are called extraneous variables.
Statistic	A statistic is an observable random variable of a sample.
Inference	Inference is the act or process of drawing a conclusion based solely on what one already knows.
Research design	A research design tests a hypothesis. The basic typess are: descriptive, correlational, and

	experimental.
Placebo effect	The placebo effect is the phenomenon that a patient's symptoms can be alleviated by an otherwise ineffective treatment, apparently because the individual expects or believes that it will work.
Placebo	Placebo refers to a bogus treatment that has the appearance of being genuine.
Statistical significance	The condition that exists when the probability that the observed findings are due to chance is very low is called statistical significance.

Abnormal behavior
An action, thought, or feeling that is harmful to the person or to others is called abnormal behavior.

Clinician
A health professional authorized to provide services to people suffering from one or more pathologies is a clinician.

Psychopathology
Psychopathology refers to the field concerned with the nature and development of mental disorders.

Maladjustment
Maladjustment is the condition of being unable to adapt properly to your environment with resulting emotional instability.

Mental illness
Mental illness is the term formerly used to mean psychological disorder but less preferred because it implies that the causes of the disorder can be found in a medical disease process.

Clinical psychology
Clinical psychology is involved in the diagnosis, assessment, and treatment of patients with mental or behavioral disorders, and conducts research in these various areas.

Clinical psychologist
A psychologist, usually with a Ph.D, whose training is in the diagnosis, treatment, or research of psychological and behavioral disorders is a clinical psychologist.

Mental disorder
Mental disorder refers to a disturbance in a person's emotions, drives, thought processes, or behavior that involves serious and relatively prolonged distress and/or impairment in ability to function, is not simply a normal response to some event or set of events in the person's environment.

Social norm
A social norm, is a rule that is socially enforced. In social situations, such as meetings, they are unwritten and often unstated rules that govern individuals' behavior. A social norm is most evident when not followed or broken.

Conformity
Conformity is the degree to which members of a group will change their behavior, views and attitudes to fit the views of the group. The group can influence members via unconscious processes or via overt social pressure on individuals.

Attention
Attention is the cognitive process of selectively concentrating on one thing while ignoring other things. Psychologists have labeled three types of attention: sustained attention, selective attention, and divided attention.

Norms
In testing, standards of test performance that permit the comparison of one person's score on the test to the scores of others who have taken the same test are referred to as norms.

Learning
Learning is a relatively permanent change in behavior that results from experience. Thus, to attribute a behavioral change to learning, the change must be relatively permanent and must result from experience.

Achievement test
A test designed to determine a person's level of knowledge in a given subject area is referred to as an achievement test.

Intelligence test
An intelligence test is a standardized means of assessing a person's current mental ability, for example, the Stanford-Binet test and the Wechsler Adult Intelligence Scale.

Mental retardation
Mental retardation refers to having significantly below-average intellectual functioning and limitations in at least two areas of adaptive functioning. Many categorize retardation as mild, moderate, severe, or profound.

Psychiatrist
A psychiatrist is a physician who specializes in the diagnosis and treatment of psychological disorders.

Schizophrenia
Schizophrenia is characterized by persistent defects in the perception or expression of reality. A person suffering from untreated schizophrenia typically demonstrates grossly disorganized thinking, and may also experience delusions or auditory hallucinations

Personality	Personality refers to the pattern of enduring characteristics that differentiates a person, the patterns of behaviors that make each individual unique.
Paranoid	The term paranoid is typically used in a general sense to signify any self-referential delusion, or more specifically, to signify a delusion involving the fear of persecution.
Quantitative	A quantitative property is one that exists in a range of magnitudes, and can therefore be measured. Measurements of any particular quantitative property are expressed as as a specific quantity, referred to as a unit, multiplied by a number.
Psychopathol-gists	Psychopathologists are mental health professionals who conduct research into the nature and development of mental disorders.
Etiology	Etiology is the study of causation. The term is used in philosophy, physics and biology in reference to the causes of various phenomena. It is generally the study of why things occur, or even the reasons behind the way that things act.
Alcohol use disorders	Cognitive, biological, behavioral, and social problems associated with alcohol use and abuse are referred to as alcohol use disorders.
Prospective study	Prospective study is a long-term study of a group of people, beginning before the onset of a common disorder. It allows investigators to see how the disorder develops.
Alcoholism	A disorder that involves long-term, repeated, uncontrolled, compulsive, and excessive use of alcoholic beverages and that impairs the drinker's health and work and social relationships is called alcoholism.
Empirical	Empirical means the use of working hypotheses which are capable of being disproved using observation or experiment.
Theories	Theories are logically self-consistent models or frameworks describing the behavior of a certain natural or social phenomenon. They are broad explanations and predictions concerning phenomena of interest.
Control subjects	Control subjects are participants in an experiment who do not receive the treatment effect but for whom all other conditions are held comparable to those of experimental subjects.
Alcoholic	An alcoholic is dependent on alcohol as characterized by craving, loss of control, physical dependence and withdrawal symptoms, and tolerance.
Variable	A variable refers to a measurable factor, characteristic, or attribute of an individual or a system.
Basic research	Basic research has as its primary objective the advancement of knowledge and the theoretical understanding of the relations among variables . It is exploratory and often driven by the researcher's curiosity, interest or hunch.
Gene	A gene is an ultramicroscopic area of the chromosome. It is the smallest physical unit of the DNA molecule that carries a piece of hereditary information.
Nonconformity	Nonconformity occurs when individuals know what people around them expect but do not use those expectations to guide their behavior.
Subculture	As understood in sociology, anthropology and cultural studies, a subculture is a set of people with a distinct set of behavior and beliefs that differentiate them from a larger culture of which they are a part.
Emotion	An emotion is a mental states that arise spontaneously, rather than through conscious effort. They are often accompanied by physiological changes.
Ethnicity	Ethnicity refers to a characteristic based on cultural heritage, nationality characteristics, race, religion, and language.

Discrimination	In Learning theory, discrimination refers the ability to distinguish between a conditioned stimulus and other stimuli. It can be brought about by extensive training or differential reinforcement. In social terms, it is the denial of privileges to a person or a group on the basis of prejudice.
Chronic	Chronic refers to a relatively long duration, usually more than a few months.
Socioeconomic	Socioeconomic pertains to the study of the social and economic impacts of any product or service offering, market intervention or other activity on an economy as a whole and on the companies, organization and individuals who are its main economic actors.
Socioeconomic Status	A family's socioeconomic status is based on family income, parental education level, parental occupation, and social status in the community. Those with high status often have more success in preparing their children for school because they have access to a wide range of resources.
Syndrome	The term syndrome is the association of several clinically recognizable features, signs, symptoms, phenomena or characteristics which often occur together, so that the presence of one feature indicates the presence of the others.
Presenting problem	The presenting problem is the original complaint reported by the client to the therapist. The actual treated problem may sometimes be a modification derived from the presenting problem or entirely different..
Perception	Perception is the process of acquiring, interpreting, selecting, and organizing sensory information.
Overt behavior	An action or response that is directly observable and measurable is an overt behavior.
Anxiety	Anxiety is a complex combination of the feeling of fear, apprehension and worry often accompanied by physical sensations such as palpitations, chest pain and/or shortness of breath.
Neurosis	Neurosis, any mental disorder that, although may cause distress, does not interfere with rational thought or the persons' ability to function.
Habit	A habit is a response that has become completely separated from its eliciting stimulus. Early learning theorists used the term to describe S-R associations, however not all S-R associations become a habit, rather many are extinguished after reinforcement is withdrawn.
Inference	Inference is the act or process of drawing a conclusion based solely on what one already knows.
Affect	A subjective feeling or emotional tone often accompanied by bodily expressions noticeable to others is called affect.
Society	The social sciences use the term society to mean a group of people that form a semi-closed (or semi-open) social system, in which most interactions are with other individuals belonging to the group.
Tumor	A tumor is an abnormal growth that when located in the brain can either be malignant and directly destroy brain tissue, or be benign and disrupt functioning by increasing intracranial pressure.
Bipolar disorder	Bipolar Disorder is a mood disorder typically characterized by fluctuations between manic and depressive states; and, more generally, atypical mood regulation and mood instability.
Hallucination	A hallucination is a sensory perception experienced in the absence of an external stimulus, as distinct from an illusion, which is a misperception of an external stimulus. They may occur in any sensory modality - visual, auditory, olfactory, gustatory, tactile, or mixed.

Delusion	A false belief, not generally shared by others, and that cannot be changed despite strong evidence to the contrary is a delusion.
Psychological test	Psychological test refers to a standardized measure of a sample of a person's behavior.
Experimental group	Experimental group refers to any group receiving a treatment effect in an experiment.
Sexual abuse	Sexual abuse is a term used to describe non- consentual sexual relations between two or more parties which are considered criminally and/or morally offensive.
Cyclothymia	Cyclothymia is a chronic mood disturbance generally lasting at least two years and characterized by mood swings including periods of hypomania and depression.
Paraphrenia	A term sometimes used to refer to schizophrenia in an older adult is paraphrenia.
Affective	Affective is the way people react emotionally, their ability to feel another living thing's pain or joy.
Psychosis	Psychosis is a generic term for mental states in which the components of rational thought and perception are severely impaired. Persons experiencing a psychosis may experience hallucinations, hold paranoid or delusional beliefs, demonstrate personality changes and exhibit disorganized thinking. This is usually accompanied by features such as a lack of insight into the unusual or bizarre nature of their behavior, difficulties with social interaction and impairments in carrying out the activities of daily living.
Paranoia	In popular culture, the term paranoia is usually used to describe excessive concern about one's own well-being, sometimes suggesting a person holds persecutory beliefs concerning a threat to themselves or their property and is often linked to a belief in conspiracy theories.
Melancholia	Melancholia was described as a distinct disease as early as the fifth and fourth centuries BC in the Hippocratic writings. It was characterized by "aversion to food, despondency, sleeplessness, irritability, restlessness," as well as the statement that "Grief and fear, when lingering, provoke melancholia". It is now generally believed that melancholia was the same phenomenon as what is now called clinical depression.
Dementia	Dementia is progressive decline in cognitive function due to damage or disease in the brain beyond what might be expected from normal aging.
Brain	The brain controls and coordinates most movement, behavior and homeostatic body functions such as heartbeat, blood pressure, fluid balance and body temperature. Functions of the brain are responsible for cognition, emotion, memory, motor learning and other sorts of learning. The brain is primarily made up of two types of cells: glia and neurons.
Personality disorder	A mental disorder characterized by a set of inflexible, maladaptive personality traits that keep a person from functioning properly in society is referred to as a personality disorder.
Prognosis	A forecast about the probable course of an illess is referred to as prognosis.
Suicide	Suicide behavior is rare in childhood but escalates in adolescence. The suicide rate increases in a linear fashion from adolescence through late adulthood.
Suicidal ideation	Suicidal ideation refers to having serious thoughts about committing suicide.
Reality testing	Reality testing is the capacity to perceive one's environment and oneself according to accurate sensory impressions.
Binge	Binge refers to relatively brief episode of uncontrolled, excessive consumption.

Obsession An obsession is a thought or idea that the sufferer cannot stop thinking about. Common examples include fears of acquiring disease, getting hurt, or causing harm to someone. They are typically automatic, frequent, distressing, and difficult to control or put an end to by themselves.

Psychotic behavior A psychotic behavior is a severe psychological disorder characterized by hallucinations and loss of contact with reality.

Major depression Major depression is characterized by a severely depressed mood that persists for at least two weeks. Episodes of depression may start suddenly or slowly and can occur several times through a person's life. The disorder may be categorized as "single episode" or "recurrent" depending on whether previous episodes have been experienced before.

Suppression Suppression is the defense mechanism where a memory is deliberately forgotten.

Depression In everyday language depression refers to any downturn in mood, which may be relatively transitory and perhaps due to something trivial. This is differentiated from Clinical depression which is marked by symptoms that last two weeks or more and are so severe that they interfere with daily living.

Vascular dementia Vascular dementia is a form of dementia resulting from brain damage caused by stroke or transient ischemic attacks (also known as mini-strokes). The specific symptoms will depend on the part of the brain damaged by the stroke or mini-stroke.

Delirium Delirium is a medical term used to describe an acute decline in attention and cognition. Delirium is probably the single most common acute disorder affecting adults in general hospitals. It affects 10-20% of all adults in hospital, and 30-40% of older patients.

Behavioral observation A form of behavioral assessment that entails careful observation of a person's overt behavior in a particular situation is behavioral observation.

Heterogeneous A heterogeneous compound, mixture, or other such object is one that consists of many different items, which are often not easily sorted or separated, though they are clearly distinct.

Homosexuality Homosexuality refers to a sexual orientation characterized by aesthetic attraction, romantic love, and sexual desire exclusively for members of the same sex or gender identity.

Reliability Reliability means the extent to which a test produces a consistent , reproducible score .

Validity The extent to which a test measures what it is intended to measure is called validity.

Bulimia Bulimia refers to a disorder in which a person binges on incredibly large quantities of food, then purges by vomiting or by using laxatives. Bulimia is often less about food, and more to do with deep psychological issues and profound feelings of lack of control.

Structured interview Structured interview refers to an interview in which the questions are set out in a prescribed fashion for the interviewer. It assists professionals in making diagnostic decisions based upon standardized criteria.

Anxiety disorder Anxiety disorder is a blanket term covering several different forms of abnormal anxiety, fear, phobia and nervous condition, that come on suddenly and prevent pursuing normal daily routines.

Generalized anxiety disorder Generalized anxiety disorder is an anxiety disorder that is characterized by uncontrollable worry about everyday things. The frequency, intensity, and duration of the worry are disproportionate to the actual source of worry, and such worry often interferes with daily functioning.

Laboratory study Any research study in which the subjects are brought to a specially designated area that has been set up to facilitate the researcher's ability to control the environment or collect data

	is referred to as a laboratory study.
Family studies	Scientific studies in which researchers assess hereditary influence by examining blood relatives to see how much they resemble each other on a specific trait are called family studies.
Construct	A generalized concept, such as anxiety or gravity, is a construct.
Bias	A bias is a prejudice in a general or specific sense, usually in the sense for having a preference to one particular point of view or ideological perspective.
Pathology	Pathology is the study of the processes underlying disease and other forms of illness, harmful abnormality, or dysfunction.
Stuttering	The term stuttering is most commonly associated with involuntary sound repetition, but it also encompasses the abnormal hesitation or pausing before speech.
Specific phobia	A specific phobia is a generic term for anxiety disorders that amount to unreasonable or irrational fear or anxiety related with exposure to specific objects or situations. As a result, the affected persons tend to actively avoid these objects or situations.
Displacement	An unconscious defense mechanism in which the individual directs aggressive or sexual feelings away from the primary object to someone or something safe is referred to as displacement. Displacement in linguistics is simply the ability to talk about things not present.
Maladaptive	In psychology, a behavior or trait is adaptive when it helps an individual adjust and function well within their social environment. A maladaptive behavior or trait is counterproductive to the individual.
Cognition	The intellectual processes through which information is obtained, transformed, stored, retrieved, and otherwise used is cognition.
Phobia	A persistent, irrational fear of an object, situation, or activity that the person feels compelled to avoid is referred to as a phobia.
Intrapsychic conflict	In psychoanalysis, the struggles among the id, ego, and superego are an intrapsychic conflict.
Conditioning	Conditioning describes the process by which behaviors can be learned or modified through interaction with the environment.
Classical conditioning	Classical conditioning is a simple form of learning in which an organism comes to associate or anticipate events. A neutral stimulus comes to evoke the response usually evoked by a natural or unconditioned stimulus by being paired repeatedly with the unconditioned stimulus.
Predisposition	Predisposition refers to an inclination or diathesis to respond in a certain way, either inborn or acquired. In abnormal psychology, it is a factor that lowers the ability to withstand stress and inclines the individual toward pathology.
Diathesis	A predisposition toward a disease or abnormality is a diathesis.
Neurotransmitter	A neurotransmitter is a chemical that is used to relay, amplify and modulate electrical signals between a neurons and another cell.
Schema	Schema refers to a way of mentally representing the world, such as a belief or an expectation, that can influence perception of persons, objects, and situations.
Dimensional classification	The dimensional classification is an approach to assessment according to which a person is placed on a continuum versus an all-or-none scale.
Psychodynamic	Most psychodynamic approaches are centered around the idea of a maladapted function developed

early in life (usually childhood) which are at least in part unconscious. This maladapted function (a.k.a. defense mechanism) does not do well in place of a normal/healthy one.

Global Assessment of Functioning

Global Assessment of Functioning is a numeric scale (0 through 100) used by mental health clinicians and doctors to rate the social, occupational and psychological functioning of adults.

Clinical psychology	Clinical psychology is involved in the diagnosis, assessment, and treatment of patients with mental or behavioral disorders, and conducts research in these various areas.
Clinical assessment	A clinical assessment is a systematic evaluation and measurement of psychological, biological, and social factors in a person presenting with a possible psychological disorder.
Psychotherapy	Psychotherapy is a set of techniques based on psychological principles intended to improve mental health, emotional or behavioral issues.
Clinician	A health professional authorized to provide services to people suffering from one or more pathologies is a clinician.
Electroencep-alogram	Electroencephalography is the neurophysiologic measurement of the electrical activity of the brain by recording from electrodes placed on the scalp, or in the special cases on the cortex. The resulting traces are known as an electroencephalogram and represent so-called brainwaves.
Neurologist	A physician who studies the nervous system, especially its structure, functions, and abnormalities is referred to as neurologist.
Encephalitis	Encephalitis is an acute inflammation of the brain, commonly caused by a viral infection.
Birth trauma	Birth trauma refers to injury or disturbing experiences sustained at the time of birth.
Trauma	Trauma refers to a severe physical injury or wound to the body caused by an external force, or a psychological shock having a lasting effect on mental life.
Attention	Attention is the cognitive process of selectively concentrating on one thing while ignoring other things. Psychologists have labeled three types of attention: sustained attention, selective attention, and divided attention.
Attention deficit/hype-activity disorder	Disorders of childhood and adolescence characterized by socially disruptive behaviors-either attentional problems or hyperactivity-that persist for at least six months are an attention deficit/hyperactivity disorder.
Personality test	A personality test aims to describe aspects of a person's character that remain stable across situations.
Personality	Personality refers to the pattern of enduring characteristics that differentiates a person, the patterns of behaviors that make each individual unique.
Psychiatrist	A psychiatrist is a physician who specializes in the diagnosis and treatment of psychological disorders.
Psychometric	Psychometric study is concerned with the theory and technique of psychological measurement, which includes the measurement of knowledge, abilities, attitudes, and personality traits. The field is primarily concerned with the study of differences between individuals
Inference	Inference is the act or process of drawing a conclusion based solely on what one already knows.
Psychodynamic	Most psychodynamic approaches are centered around the idea of a maladapted function developed early in life (usually childhood) which are at least in part unconscious. This maladapted function (a.k.a. defense mechanism) does not do well in place of a normal/healthy one.
Projective test	A projective test is a personality test designed to let a person respond to ambiguous stimuli, presumably revealing hidden emotions and internal conflicts. This is different from an "objective test" in which responses are analyzed according to a universal standard rather than an individual psychiatrist's judgement.
Clinical	A psychologist, usually with a Ph.D, whose training is in the diagnosis, treatment, or

psychologist	research of psychological and behavioral disorders is a clinical psychologist.
Psychological test	Psychological test refers to a standardized measure of a sample of a person's behavior.
Mental disorder	Mental disorder refers to a disturbance in a person's emotions, drives, thought processes, or behavior that involves serious and relatively prolonged distress and/or impairment in ability to function, is not simply a normal response to some event or set of events in the person's environment.
Reliability	Reliability means the extent to which a test produces a consistent , reproducible score .
Behavioral assessment	Direct measures of an individual's behavior used to describe characteristics indicative of personality are called behavioral assessment.
Psychological testing	Psychological testing is a field characterized by the use of small samples of behavior in order to infer larger generalizations about a given individual. The technical term for psychological testing is psychometrics.
Depression	In everyday language depression refers to any downturn in mood, which may be relatively transitory and perhaps due to something trivial. This is differentiated from Clinical depression which is marked by symptoms that last two weeks or more and are so severe that they interfere with daily living.
Feedback	Feedback refers to information returned to a person about the effects a response has had.
Threshold	In general, a threshold is a fixed location or value where an abrupt change is observed. In the sensory modalities, it is the minimum amount of stimulus energy necessary to elicit a sensory response.
Clinical significance	The degree to which research findings have useful and meaningful applications to real problems is called their clinical significance.
Compulsion	An apparently irresistible urge to repeat an act or engage in ritualistic behavior such as hand washing is referred to as a compulsion.
Informed consent	The term used by psychologists to indicate that a person has agreed to participate in research after receiving information about the purposes of the study and the nature of the treatments is informed consent. Even with informed consent, subjects may withdraw from any experiment at any time.
Positive relationship	Statistically, a positive relationship refers to a mathematical relationship in which increases in one measure are matched by increases in the other.
Anxiety	Anxiety is a complex combination of the feeling of fear, apprehension and worry often accompanied by physical sensations such as palpitations, chest pain and/or shortness of breath.
Attitude	An enduring mental representation of a person, place, or thing that evokes an emotional response and related behavior is called attitude.
Empathy	Empathy is the recognition and understanding of the states of mind, including beliefs, desires and particularly emotions of others without injecting your own.
Assertiveness	Assertiveness basically means the ability to express your thoughts and feelings in a way that clearly states your needs and keeps the lines of communication open with the other.
Hypothesis	A specific statement about behavior or mental processes that is testable through research is a hypothesis.
Perception	Perception is the process of acquiring, interpreting, selecting, and organizing sensory information.

Affect	A subjective feeling or emotional tone often accompanied by bodily expressions noticeable to others is called affect.
Pathology	Pathology is the study of the processes underlying disease and other forms of illness, harmful abnormality, or dysfunction.
Psychosis	Psychosis is a generic term for mental states in which the components of rational thought and perception are severely impaired. Persons experiencing a psychosis may experience hallucinations, hold paranoid or delusional beliefs, demonstrate personality changes and exhibit disorganized thinking. This is usually accompanied by features such as a lack of insight into the unusual or bizarre nature of their behavior, difficulties with social interaction and impairments in carrying out the activities of daily living.
Gender difference	A gender difference is a disparity between genders involving quality or quantity. Though some gender differences are controversial, they are not to be confused with sexist stereotypes.
Sexual orientation	Sexual orientation refers to the sex or gender of people who are the focus of a person's amorous or erotic desires, fantasies, and spontaneous feelings, the gender(s) toward which one is primarily "oriented".
Structured interview	Structured interview refers to an interview in which the questions are set out in a prescribed fashion for the interviewer. It assists professionals in making diagnostic decisions based upon standardized criteria.
Motivation	In psychology, motivation is the driving force (desire) behind all actions of an organism.
Psychiatric social worker	A mental health professional trained to apply social science principles to help patients in clinics and hospitals is the psychiatric social worker.
Presenting problem	The presenting problem is the original complaint reported by the client to the therapist. The actual treated problem may sometimes be a modification derived from the presenting problem or entirely different..
Substance abuse	Substance abuse refers to the overindulgence in and dependence on a stimulant, depressant, or other chemical substance, leading to effects that are detrimental to the individual's physical or mental health, or the welfare of others.
Hallucination	A hallucination is a sensory perception experienced in the absence of an external stimulus, as distinct from an illusion, which is a misperception of an external stimulus. They may occur in any sensory modality - visual, auditory, olfactory, gustatory, tactile, or mixed.
Delusion	A false belief, not generally shared by others, and that cannot be changed despite strong evidence to the contrary is a delusion.
Insight	Insight refers to a sudden awareness of the relationships among various elements that had previously appeared to be independent of one another.
Etiology	Etiology is the study of causation. The term is used in philosophy, physics and biology in reference to the causes of various phenomena. It is generally the study of why things occur, or even the reasons behind the way that things act.
Mania	Mania is a medical condition characterized by severely elevated mood. Mania is most usually associated with bipolar disorder, where episodes of mania may cyclically alternate with episodes of depression.
Validity	The extent to which a test measures what it is intended to measure is called validity.
Diagnostic and Statistical Manual of Mental	The Diagnostic and Statistical Manual of Mental Disorders, published by the American Psychiatric Association, is the handbook used most often in diagnosing mental disorders in the United States and internationally.

Disorders	
Beck	Beck was initially trained as a psychoanalyst and conducted research on the psychoanalytic treatment of depression. With out the strong ability to collect data to this end, he began exploring cognitive approaches to treatment and originated cognitive behavior therapy.
Correlation	A statistical technique for determining the degree of association between two or more variables is referred to as correlation.
Correlation coefficient	Correlation coefficient refers to a number from +1.00 to -1.00 that expresses the direction and extent of the relationship between two variables. The closer to 1, the stronger the relationship. The sign, + or -, indicates the direction.
Construct	A generalized concept, such as anxiety or gravity, is a construct.
Predictive validity	Predictive validity refers to the relation between test scores and the student 's future performance .
Variance	The degree to which scores differ among individuals in a distribution of scores is the variance.
Specific phobia	A specific phobia is a generic term for anxiety disorders that amount to unreasonable or irrational fear or anxiety related with exposure to specific objects or situations. As a result, the affected persons tend to actively avoid these objects or situations.
Phobia	A persistent, irrational fear of an object, situation, or activity that the person feels compelled to avoid is referred to as a phobia.
Panic attack	An attack of overwhelming anxiety, fear, or terror is called panic attack.
Stimulus	A change in an environmental condition that elicits a response is a stimulus.
Separation anxiety	Separation anxiety is a psychological condition in which an individual has excessive anxiety regarding separation from home, or from those with whom the individual has a strong attachment.
Anxiety disorder	Anxiety disorder is a blanket term covering several different forms of abnormal anxiety, fear, phobia and nervous condition, that come on suddenly and prevent pursuing normal daily routines.
Stress disorder	A significant emotional disturbance caused by stresses outside the range of normal human experience is referred to as stress disorder.
Panic disorder	A panic attack is a period of intense fear or discomfort, typically with an abrupt onset and usually lasting no more than thirty minutes. The disorder is strikingly different from other types of anxiety, in that panic attacks are very sudden, appear to be unprovoked, and are often disabling. People who have repeated attacks, or feel severe anxiety about having another attack are said to have panic disorder.
Social phobia	An irrational, excessive fear of public scrutiny is referred to as social phobia.
Agoraphobia	An irrational fear of open, crowded places is called agoraphobia. Many people suffering from agoraphobia, however, are not afraid of the open spaces themselves, but of situations often associated with these spaces, such as social gatherings.
Panic disorder with agoraphobia	In panic disorder with agoraphobia the person may experience severe panic attacks during situations where they feel trapped, insecure, out of control, or too far from their personal comfort zone. During severe bouts of anxiety, the person is confined not only to their home, but to one or two rooms and they may even become bedbound until their over-stimulated nervous system can quiet down, and their adrenaline levels return to a more normal level.
Separation	Separation anxiety disorder is a psychological condition in which an individual has excessive

anxiety disorder	anxiety regarding separation from home, or from those with whom the individual has a strong attachment.
Interrater reliability	Interrater reliability is the correlation between ratings of two or more raters in a given research study.
Major depressive episode	A major depressive episode is a common and severe experience of depression. It includes feelings of worthlessness, disturbances in bodily activities such as sleep, loss of interest, and the inability to experience pleasure. It lasts for at least two weeks.
Variable	A variable refers to a measurable factor, characteristic, or attribute of an individual or a system.
Syndrome	The term syndrome is the association of several clinically recognizable features, signs, symptoms, phenomena or characteristics which often occur together, so that the presence of one feature indicates the presence of the others.
Personality trait	According to the Diagnostic and Statistical Manual of the American Psychiatric Association, a personality trait is a "prominent aspect of personality that is exhibited in a wide range of important social and personal contexts. ...".
Trait	An enduring personality characteristic that tends to lead to certain behaviors is called a trait. The term trait also means a genetically inherited feature of an organism.
Alcoholism	A disorder that involves long-term, repeated, uncontrolled, compulsive, and excessive use of alcoholic beverages and that impairs the drinker's health and work and social relationships is called alcoholism.
Content validity	The degree to which the content of a test is representative of the domain it's supposed to cover is referred to as its content validity.
Discriminant validity	Discriminant validity shows that a measure doesn't measure what it isn't meant to measure, it discriminates.
Construct validity	The extent to which there is evidence that a test measures a particular hypothetical construct is referred to as construct validity.
Representative sample	Representative sample refers to a sample of participants selected from the larger population in such a way that important subgroups within the population are included in the sample in the same proportions as they are found in the larger population.
Motives	Needs or desires that energize and direct behavior toward a goal are motives.
Cultural values	The importance and desirability of various objects and activities as defined by people in a given culture are referred to as cultural values.
Psychopathology	Psychopathology refers to the field concerned with the nature and development of mental disorders.
Theories	Theories are logically self-consistent models or frameworks describing the behavior of a certain natural or social phenomenon. They are broad explanations and predictions concerning phenomena of interest.
Illusion	An illusion is a distortion of a sensory perception.
Concurrent validity	Concurrent validity is demonstrated where a test correlates well with a measure that has previously been validated.
Problem solving	An attempt to find an appropriate way of attaining a goal when the goal is not readily available is called problem solving.

Clinical psychology	Clinical psychology is involved in the diagnosis, assessment, and treatment of patients with mental or behavioral disorders, and conducts research in these various areas.
Clinician	A health professional authorized to provide services to people suffering from one or more pathologies is a clinician.
Thorndike	Thorndike worked in animal behavior and the learning process leading to the theory of connectionism. Among his most famous contributions were his research on cats escaping from puzzle boxes, and his formulation of the Law of Effect.
Reaction time	The amount of time required to respond to a stimulus is referred to as reaction time.
Galton	Galton was one of the first experimental psychologists, and the founder of the field of Differential Psychology, which concerns itself with individual differences rather than on common trends. He created the statistical methods correlation and regression.
James McKeen Cattell	James McKeen Cattell was the first professor of psychology in the United States. His major contribution to psychology was the realization of the importance, and subsequent implementation, of quantitative methodologies and techniques. He coined the term "mental test" 1890.
Theodore Simon	Theodore Simon co-created the Stanford-Binet Intelligence Scale test with Alfred Binet.
Alfred Binet	Alfred Binet published the first modern intelligence test, the Binet-Simon intelligence scale, in 1905. Binet stressed that the core of intelligence consists of complex cognitive processes, such as memory, imagery, comprehension, and judgment; and, that these developed over time in the individual.
Individual differences	Individual differences psychology studies the ways in which individual people differ in their behavior. This is distinguished from other aspects of psychology in that although psychology is ostensibly a study of individuals, modern psychologists invariably study groups.
Intelligence test	An intelligence test is a standardized means of assessing a person's current mental ability, for example, the Stanford-Binet test and the Wechsler Adult Intelligence Scale.
Herrnstein	Herrnstein was a prominent researcher in comparative psychology who did pioneering work on pigeon intelligence employing the Experimental Analysis of Behavior and formulated the "Matching Law" in the 1960s, a breakthrough in understanding how reinforcement and behavior are linked.
Affect	A subjective feeling or emotional tone often accompanied by bodily expressions noticeable to others is called affect.
Psychological test	Psychological test refers to a standardized measure of a sample of a person's behavior.
Reliability	Reliability means the extent to which a test produces a consistent , reproducible score .
Validity	The extent to which a test measures what it is intended to measure is called validity.
Gene	A gene is an ultramicroscopic area of the chromosome. It is the smallest physical unit of the DNA molecule that carries a piece of hereditary information.
Social policy	Social policy is the study of the welfare state, and the range of responses to social need.
Empirical	Empirical means the use of working hypotheses which are capable of being disproved using observation or experiment.
Practice effects	Practice effects are the effects brought about by the continued repetition of a task.
Construct	A generalized concept, such as anxiety or gravity, is a construct.
Internal	Internal consistency reliability is the level of agreement among the items in a test and the

consistency reliability	level of agreement of multiple ratings by different raters.
Content validity	The degree to which the content of a test is representative of the domain it's supposed to cover is referred to as its content validity.
Variable	A variable refers to a measurable factor, characteristic, or attribute of an individual or a system.
Predictive validity	Predictive validity refers to the relation between test scores and the student 's future performance .
Construct validity	The extent to which there is evidence that a test measures a particular hypothetical construct is referred to as construct validity.
Concurrent validity	Concurrent validity is demonstrated where a test correlates well with a measure that has previously been validated.
Depression	In everyday language depression refers to any downturn in mood, which may be relatively transitory and perhaps due to something trivial. This is differentiated from Clinical depression which is marked by symptoms that last two weeks or more and are so severe that they interfere with daily living.
Achievement test	A test designed to determine a person's level of knowledge in a given subject area is referred to as an achievement test.
Inference	Inference is the act or process of drawing a conclusion based solely on what one already knows.
Wechsler	Wechsler is best known for his intelligence tests. The Wechsler Adult Intelligence Scale (WAIS) was developed first in 1939 and then called the Wechsler-Bellevue Intelligence Test. From these he derived the Wechsler Intelligence Scale for Children (WISC) in 1949 and the Wechsler Preschool and Primary Scale of Intelligence (WPPSI) in 1967. Wechsler originally created these tests to find out more about his patients at the Bellevue clinic and he found the then-current Binet IQ test unsatisfactory.
Insight	Insight refers to a sudden awareness of the relationships among various elements that had previously appeared to be independent of one another.
Norms	In testing, standards of test performance that permit the comparison of one person's score on the test to the scores of others who have taken the same test are referred to as norms.
Sternberg	Sternberg proposed the triarchic theory of intelligence: componential, experiential, and practical. His notion of general intelligence or the g-factor, is a composite of intelligence scores across multiple modalities.
Learning	Learning is a relatively permanent change in behavior that results from experience. Thus, to attribute a behavioral change to learning, the change must be relatively permanent and must result from experience.
Prototype	A concept of a category of objects or events that serves as a good example of the category is called a prototype.
Trait	An enduring personality characteristic that tends to lead to certain behaviors is called a trait. The term trait also means a genetically inherited feature of an organism.
Theories	Theories are logically self-consistent models or frameworks describing the behavior of a certain natural or social phenomenon. They are broad explanations and predictions concerning phenomena of interest.
Factor analysis	Factor analysis is a statistical technique that originated in psychometrics. The objective is

	to explain the most of the variability among a number of observable random variables in terms of a smaller number of unobservable random variables called factors.
G factor	Spearman's term for a general intellectual ability that underlies all mental operations to some degree is called the g factor.
Thurstone	Thurstone was a pioneer in the field of psychometrics. His work in factor analysis led him to formulate a model of intelligence center around "Primary Mental Abilities", which were independent group factors of intelligence that different individuals possessed in varying degrees.
Reasoning	Reasoning is the act of using reason to derive a conclusion from certain premises. There are two main methods to reach a conclusion,deductive reasoning and inductive reasoning.
Primary mental abilities	According to Thurstone, the basic abilities that make up intelligence are called primary mental abilities.
Guilford	Guilford observed that most individuals display a preference for either convergent or divergent thinking. Scientists and engineers typically prefer the former and artists and performers, the latter.
Cognition	The intellectual processes through which information is obtained, transformed, stored, retrieved, and otherwise used is cognition.
Convergent production	Convergent production is the deductive generation of the best single answer to a set problem, usually where there is a compelling inference.
Divergent production	Divergent production is the creative generation of multiple answers to a set problem.
Information processing	Information processing is an approach to the goal of understanding human thinking. The essence of the approach is to see cognition as being essentially computational in nature, with mind being the software and the brain being the hardware.
Theory of multiple intelligences	Gardner's theory of multiple intelligences suggests several different kinds of "intelligence" exist in humans, each relating to a different sphere of human life and activity. .
Attention	Attention is the cognitive process of selectively concentrating on one thing while ignoring other things. Psychologists have labeled three types of attention: sustained attention, selective attention, and divided attention.
Triarchic theory	Sternberg's theory that there are three main types of intelligence: analytical, creative, and practical is called the triarchic theory of intelligence.
Triarchic Theory of Intelligence	The Triarchic Theory of Intelligence was formulated by Robert J. Sternberg. It proposes that intelligence consists of componential intelligence, experiential intelligence, and contextual intelligence.
Creative thinking	Creative thinking is a mental process involving the generation of new ideas or concepts, or new associations between existing ideas or concepts. From a scientific point of view, the products of are usually considered to have both originality and appropriateness.
Mental age	The mental age refers to the accumulated months of credit that a person earns on the Stanford-Binet Intelligence Scale.
Intelligence quotient	An intelligence quotient is a score derived from a set of standardized tests that were developed with the purpose of measuring a person's cognitive abilities ("intelligence") in relation to their age group.
Chronological	Chronological age refers to the number of years that have elapsed since a person's birth.

age	
Population	Population refers to all members of a well-defined group of organisms, events, or things.
IQ test	An IQ test is a standardized test developed to measure a person's cognitive abilities ("intelligence") in relation to their age group.
Society	The social sciences use the term society to mean a group of people that form a semi-closed (or semi-open) social system, in which most interactions are with other individuals belonging to the group.
Correlation	A statistical technique for determining the degree of association between two or more variables is referred to as correlation.
Motivation	In psychology, motivation is the driving force (desire) behind all actions of an organism.
Attitude	An enduring mental representation of a person, place, or thing that evokes an emotional response and related behavior is called attitude.
Quantitative	A quantitative property is one that exists in a range of magnitudes, and can therefore be measured. Measurements of any particular quantitative property are expressed as as a specific quantity, referred to as a unit, multiplied by a number.
Puberty	Puberty refers to the process of physical changes by which a child's body becomes an adult body capable of reproduction.
Heritability	Heritability It is that proportion of the observed variation in a particular phenotype within a particular population, that can be attributed to the contribution of genotype. In other words: it measures the extent to which differences between individuals in a population are due their being different genetically.
Heredity	Heredity is the transfer of characteristics from parent to offspring through their genes.
Empirical evidence	Facts or information based on direct observation or experience are referred to as empirical evidence.
Genetics	Genetics is the science of genes, heredity, and the variation of organisms.
Behavioral genetics	Behavioral genetics is the field of biology that studies the role of genetics in behavior.
Monozygotic	Identical twins occur when a single egg is fertilized to form one zygote, calld monozygotic, but the zygote then divides into two separate embryos. The two embryos develop into foetuses sharing the same womb. Monozygotic twins are genetically identical unless there has been a mutation in development, and they are almost always the same gender.
Dizygotic	Fraternal twins (commonly known as "non-identical twins") usually occur when two fertilized eggs are implanted in the uterine wall at the same time. The two eggs form two zygotes, and these twins are therefore also known as dizygotic.
Adoption studies	Research studies that assess hereditary influence by examining the resemblance between adopted children and both their biological and their adoptive parents are referred to as adoption studies. The studies have been inconclusive about the relative importance of heredity in intelligence.
Variance	The degree to which scores differ among individuals in a distribution of scores is the variance.
Neurotransmitter	A neurotransmitter is a chemical that is used to relay, amplify and modulate electrical signals between a neurons and another cell.
Nervous system	The body's electrochemical communication circuitry, made up of billions of neurons is a

nervous system.

Genetic code — The genetic code is a set of rules, which maps DNA sequences to proteins in the living cell, and is employed in the process of protein synthesis. Nearly all living things use the same genetic code, called the standard genetic code, although a few organisms use minor variations of the standard code.

Genotype — The genotype is the specific genetic makeup of an individual, usually in the form of DNA. It codes for the phenotype of that individual. Any given gene will usually cause an observable change in an organism, known as the phenotype.

Hormone — A hormone is a chemical messenger from one cell (or group of cells) to another. The best known are those produced by endocrine glands, but they are produced by nearly every organ system. The function of hormones is to serve as a signal to the target cells; the action of the hormone is determined by the pattern of secretion and the signal transduction of the receiving tissue.

Protein — A protein is a complex, high-molecular-weight organic compound that consists of amino acids joined by peptide bonds. It is essential to the structure and function of all living cells and viruses. Many are enzymes or subunits of enzymes.

Phenotype — The phenotype of an individual organism is either its total physical appearance and constitution, or a specific manifestation of a trait, such as size or eye color, that varies between individuals. Phenotype is determined to some extent by genotype, or by the identity of the alleles that an individual carries at one or more positions on the chromosomes.

Mental disorder — Mental disorder refers to a disturbance in a person's emotions, drives, thought processes, or behavior that involves serious and relatively prolonged distress and/or impairment in ability to function, is not simply a normal response to some event or set of events in the person's environment.

Research design — A research design tests a hypothesis. The basic typess are: descriptive, correlational, and experimental.

Concordance — Concordance as used in genetics means the presence of the same trait in both members of a pair of twins, or in sets of individuals. A twin study examines the concordance rates of twins having the same trait, especially a disease, which can help determine how much the disease is affected by genetics versus environment.

Ethnic group — An ethnic group is a culture or subculture whose members are readily distinguishable by outsiders based on traits originating from a common racial, national, linguistic, or religious source. Members of an ethnic group are often presumed to be culturally or biologically similar, although this is not in fact necessarily the case.

Bias — A bias is a prejudice in a general or specific sense, usually in the sense for having a preference to one particular point of view or ideological perspective.

Wechsler Scales — The Wechsler Scales are two well-known intelligence scales, namely the Wechsler Adult Intelligence Scale and the Wechsler Intelligence Scale for Children.

Wechsler Adult Intelligence Scale — Wechsler adult intelligence scale is an individual intelligence test for adults that yields separate verbal and performance IQ scores as well as an overall IQ score.

Wechsler adult Intelligence — Wechsler adult Intelligence Scale is a revision of the Wechsler-Bellevue test (1939), standardized for use with adults over the age of 16.

Stimulus — A change in an environmental condition that elicits a response is a stimulus.

Raw score — A raw score is an original datum that has not been transformed – for example, the original

result obtained by a student on a test (i.e., the number of correctly answered items) as opposed to that score after transformation to a standard score or percentile rank or the like.

Working Memory — Working memory is the collection of structures and processes in the brain used for temporarily storing and manipulating information. Working memory consists of both memory for items that are currently being processed, and components governing attention and directing the processing itself.

Variability — Statistically, variability refers to how much the scores in a distribution spread out, away from the mean.

Wechsler Intelligence Scale for Children — The Wechsler Intelligence Scale for Children is an intelligence test that can be completed without reading or writing. It generates an IQ score. It also generates four composite scores; Verbal Comprehension, Perceptual Reasoning, Processing Speed and Working Memory.

Coding — In senation, coding is the process by which information about the quality and quantity of a stimulus is preserved in the pattern of action potentials sent through sensory neurons to the central nervous system.

Consciousness — The awareness of the sensations, thoughts, and feelings being experienced at a given moment is called consciousness.

Normative — The term normative is used to describe the effects of those structures of culture which regulate the function of social activity.

Learning disability — A learning disability exists when there is a significant discrepancy between one's ability and achievement.

Baseline — Measure of a particular behavior or process taken before the introduction of the independent variable or treatment is called the baseline.

Early childhood — Early childhood refers to the developmental period extending from the end of infancy to about 5 or 6 years of age; sometimes called the preschool years.

Individual intelligence test — A test of intelligence designed to be given to a single individual by a trained specialist is an individual intelligence test. Background information supplements the test.

Personality — Personality refers to the pattern of enduring characteristics that differentiates a person, the patterns of behaviors that make each individual unique.

Innate — Innate behavior is not learned or influenced by the environment, rather, it is present or predisposed at birth.

Socioeconomic — Socioeconomic pertains to the study of the social and economic impacts of any product or service offering, market intervention or other activity on an economy as a whole and on the companies, organization and individuals who are its main economic actors.

Socioeconomic Status — A family's socioeconomic status is based on family income, parental education level, parental occupation, and social status in the community. Those with high status often have more success in preparing their children for school because they have access to a wide range of resources.

Clinical psychologist — A psychologist, usually with a Ph.D, whose training is in the diagnosis, treatment, or research of psychological and behavioral disorders is a clinical psychologist.

General intelligence factor — The general intelligence factor is a widely accepted but controversial construct used in the field of psychology to quantify what is common to the scores of all intelligence tests.

Fraternal twins	Fraternal twins usually occur when two fertilized eggs are implanted in the uterine wall at the same time. The two eggs form two zygotes, and these twins are therefore also known as dizygotic. Dizygotic twins are no more similar genetically than any siblings.
Cronbach	Cronbach is most famous for the development of Cronbach's alpha, a method for determining the reliability of educational and psychological tests. His work on test reliability reached an acme with the creation of generalizability theory, a statistical model for identifying and quantifying the sources of measurement error.
Identical twins	Identical twins occur when a single egg is fertilized to form one zygote (monozygotic) but the zygote then divides into two separate embryos. The two embryos develop into foetuses sharing the same womb. Monozygotic twins are genetically identical unless there has been a mutation in development, and they are almost always the same gender.

Reliability	Reliability means the extent to which a test produces a consistent , reproducible score .
Personality	Personality refers to the pattern of enduring characteristics that differentiates a person, the patterns of behaviors that make each individual unique.
Validity	The extent to which a test measures what it is intended to measure is called validity.
Clinical psychologist	A psychologist, usually with a Ph.D, whose training is in the diagnosis, treatment, or research of psychological and behavioral disorders is a clinical psychologist.
Watson	Watson, the father of behaviorism, developed the term "Behaviorism" as a name for his proposal to revolutionize the study of human psychology in order to put it on a firm experimental footing.
Clinical psychology	Clinical psychology is involved in the diagnosis, assessment, and treatment of patients with mental or behavioral disorders, and conducts research in these various areas.
Trait	An enduring personality characteristic that tends to lead to certain behaviors is called a trait. The term trait also means a genetically inherited feature of an organism.
Projective test	A projective test is a personality test designed to let a person respond to ambiguous stimuli, presumably revealing hidden emotions and internal conflicts. This is different from an "objective test" in which responses are analyzed according to a universal standard rather than an individual psychiatrist's judgement.
Clinician	A health professional authorized to provide services to people suffering from one or more pathologies is a clinician.
Motives	Needs or desires that energize and direct behavior toward a goal are motives.
Cognition	The intellectual processes through which information is obtained, transformed, stored, retrieved, and otherwise used is cognition.
Personality trait	According to the Diagnostic and Statistical Manual of the American Psychiatric Association, a personality trait is a "prominent aspect of personality that is exhibited in a wide range of important social and personal contexts. ...".
Construct	A generalized concept, such as anxiety or gravity, is a construct.
Attention	Attention is the cognitive process of selectively concentrating on one thing while ignoring other things. Psychologists have labeled three types of attention: sustained attention, selective attention, and divided attention.
Maladjustment	Maladjustment is the condition of being unable to adapt properly to your environment with resulting emotional instability.
Content validity	The degree to which the content of a test is representative of the domain it's supposed to cover is referred to as its content validity.
Empirical	Empirical means the use of working hypotheses which are capable of being disproved using observation or experiment.
Minnesota Multiphasic Personality Inventory	The Minnesota Multiphasic Personality Inventory is the most frequently used test in the mental health fields. This assessment or test helps identify personal, social, and behavioral problems in psychiatric patients. This test helps provide relevant information to aid in problem identification, diagnosis, and treatment planning for the patient.
Personality inventory	A self-report questionnaire by which an examinee indicates whether statements assessing habitual tendencies apply to him or her is referred to as a personality inventory.
Psychopathology	Psychopathology refers to the field concerned with the nature and development of mental disorders.

Schizophrenia	Schizophrenia is characterized by persistent defects in the perception or expression of reality. A person suffering from untreated schizophrenia typically demonstrates grossly disorganized thinking, and may also experience delusions or auditory hallucinations
Factor analysis	Factor analysis is a statistical technique that originated in psychometrics. The objective is to explain the most of the variability among a number of observable random variables in terms of a smaller number of unobservable random variables called factors.
Depression	In everyday language depression refers to any downturn in mood, which may be relatively transitory and perhaps due to something trivial. This is differentiated from Clinical depression which is marked by symptoms that last two weeks or more and are so severe that they interfere with daily living.
Syndrome	The term syndrome is the association of several clinically recognizable features, signs, symptoms, phenomena or characteristics which often occur together, so that the presence of one feature indicates the presence of the others.
Homogeneous	In biology homogeneous has a meaning similar to its meaning in mathematics. Generally it means "the same" or "of the same quality or general property".
Variable	A variable refers to a measurable factor, characteristic, or attribute of an individual or a system.
Construct validity	The extent to which there is evidence that a test measures a particular hypothetical construct is referred to as construct validity.
Psychosis	Psychosis is a generic term for mental states in which the components of rational thought and perception are severely impaired. Persons experiencing a psychosis may experience hallucinations, hold paranoid or delusional beliefs, demonstrate personality changes and exhibit disorganized thinking. This is usually accompanied by features such as a lack of insight into the unusual or bizarre nature of their behavior, difficulties with social interaction and impairments in carrying out the activities of daily living.
Graham	Graham has conducted a number of studies that reveal stronger socioeconomic-status influences rather than ethnic influences in achievement.
Introversion	A personality trait characterized by intense imagination and a tendency to inhibit impulses is called introversion.
Masculinity	Masculinity is a culturally determined value reflecting the set of characteristics of maleness.
Hypomania	Hypomania is a state involving combinations of: elevated mood, irritability, racing thoughts, people-seeking, hypersexuality, grandiose thinking, religiosity, and pressured speech.
Population	Population refers to all members of a well-defined group of organisms, events, or things.
Emotion	An emotion is a mental states that arise spontaneously, rather than through conscious effort. They are often accompanied by physiological changes.
Flight of ideas	Flight of ideas is a symptom of mania that involves a rapid shift in conversation from one subject to another with only superficial associative connections.
Hallucination	A hallucination is a sensory perception experienced in the absence of an external stimulus, as distinct from an illusion, which is a misperception of an external stimulus. They may occur in any sensory modality - visual, auditory, olfactory, gustatory, tactile, or mixed.
Obsession	An obsession is a thought or idea that the sufferer cannot stop thinking about. Common examples include fears of acquiring disease, getting hurt, or causing harm to someone. They are typically automatic, frequent, distressing, and difficult to control or put an end to by themselves.

Paranoia	In popular culture, the term paranoia is usually used to describe excessive concern about one's own well-being, sometimes suggesting a person holds persecutory beliefs concerning a threat to themselves or their property and is often linked to a belief in conspiracy theories.
Delusion	A false belief, not generally shared by others, and that cannot be changed despite strong evidence to the contrary is a delusion.
Shyness	A tendency to avoid others plus uneasiness and strain when socializing is called shyness.
Guilt	Guilt describes many concepts related to a negative emotion or condition caused by actions which are believed to be, morally wrong. According to Freud, the avoidance of guilt is the basis for moral behavior.
Delusions of grandeur	Delusions of grandeur are a false belief that one is a famous person or a person who has some great knowledge, ability, or authority.
Malingering	Malingering is a medical and psychological term that refers to an individual faking the symptoms of mental or physical disorders for a myriad of reasons such as fraud, dereliction of responsibilities, attempting to obtain medications or to lighten criminal sentences.
Empirical evidence	Facts or information based on direct observation or experience are referred to as empirical evidence.
Counselor	A counselor is a mental health professional who specializes in helping people with problems not involving serious mental disorders.
Response set	A tendency to answer test items according to a personal or situational bias is called response set.
Paranoid	The term paranoid is typically used in a general sense to signify any self-referential delusion, or more specifically, to signify a delusion involving the fear of persecution.
Paranoid schizophrenia	Paranoid schizophrenia is a type of schizophrenia characterized primarily by delusions-commonly of persecution-and by vivid hallucinations .
Attitude	An enduring mental representation of a person, place, or thing that evokes an emotional response and related behavior is called attitude.
Type A personality	Type A personality is a term used to describe people who are driven, hard-working, busy, and impatient. It was first described as an important risk factor in coronary disease in the 1950's by cardiologist Meyer Friedman and his co-workers.
Situational determinants	The environmental conditions that precede and follow a particular piece of behavior, a primary focus of behavioral assessment are situational determinants.
Threshold	In general, a threshold is a fixed location or value where an abrupt change is observed. In the sensory modalities, it is the minimum amount of stimulus energy necessary to elicit a sensory response.
Normative	The term normative is used to describe the effects of those structures of culture which regulate the function of social activity.
Society	The social sciences use the term society to mean a group of people that form a semi-closed (or semi-open) social system, in which most interactions are with other individuals belonging to the group.
Bias	A bias is a prejudice in a general or specific sense, usually in the sense for having a preference to one particular point of view or ideological perspective.
Variance	The degree to which scores differ among individuals in a distribution of scores is the variance.

Conscientiousness	Conscientiousness is one of the dimensions of the five-factor model of personality and individual differences involving being organized, thorough, and reliable as opposed to careless, negligent, and unreliable.
Agreeableness	Agreeableness, one of the big-five personality traits, reflects individual differences in concern with cooperation and social harmony. It is the degree individuals value getting along with others.
Extraversion	Extraversion, one of the big-five personailty traits, is marked by pronounced engagement with the external world. They are people who enjoy being with people, are full of energy, and often experience positive emotions.
Neuroticism	Eysenck's use of the term neuroticism (or Emotional Stability) was proposed as the dimension describing individual differences in the predisposition towards neurotic disorder.
Openness to Experience	Openness to Experience, one of the big-five traits, describes a dimension of cognitive style that distinguishes imaginative, creative people from down-to-earth, conventional people.
Assertiveness	Assertiveness basically means the ability to express your thoughts and feelings in a way that clearly states your needs and keeps the lines of communication open with the other.
Altruism	Altruism is being helpful to other people with little or no interest in being rewarded for one's efforts. This is distinct from merely helping others.
Norms	In testing, standards of test performance that permit the comparison of one person's score on the test to the scores of others who have taken the same test are referred to as norms.
Projection	Attributing one's own undesirable thoughts, impulses, traits, or behaviors to others is referred to as projection.
Maladaptive	In psychology, a behavior or trait is adaptive when it helps an individual adjust and function well within their social environment. A maladaptive behavior or trait is counterproductive to the individual.
Anxiety	Anxiety is a complex combination of the feeling of fear, apprehension and worry often accompanied by physical sensations such as palpitations, chest pain and/or shortness of breath.
Personality disorder	A mental disorder characterized by a set of inflexible, maladaptive personality traits that keep a person from functioning properly in society is referred to as a personality disorder.
Clinical assessment	A clinical assessment is a systematic evaluation and measurement of psychological, biological, and social factors in a person presenting with a possible psychological disorder.
Sexual abuse	Sexual abuse is a term used to describe non- consentual sexual relations between two or more parties which are considered criminally and/or morally offensive.
Labile	Easily emotionally moved, quickly shifting from one emotion to another, or easily aroused is referred to as labile.
Transference	Transference is a phenomenon in psychology characterized by unconscious redirection of feelings from one person to another.
Mental disorder	Mental disorder refers to a disturbance in a person's emotions, drives, thought processes, or behavior that involves serious and relatively prolonged distress and/or impairment in ability to function, is not simply a normal response to some event or set of events in the person's environment.
William Stern	William Stern developed the original formula for the Intelligence Quotient (IQ) after studying the scores on Binet's intelligence test.
Rorschach	The Rorschach inkblot test is a method of psychological evaluation. It is a projective test

	associated with the Freudian school of thought. Psychologists use this test to try to probe the unconscious minds of their patients.
Kraepelin	Kraepelin postulated that there is a specific brain or other biological pathology underlying each of the major psychiatric disorders. Just as his laboratory discovered the pathologic basis of what is now known as Alzheimers disease, Kraepelin was confident that it would someday be possible to identify the pathologic basis of each of the major psychiatric disorders.
Galton	Galton was one of the first experimental psychologists, and the founder of the field of Differential Psychology, which concerns itself with individual differences rather than on common trends. He created the statistical methods correlation and regression.
Adler	Adler argued that human personality could be explained teleologically, separate strands dominated by the guiding purpose of the individual's unconscious self ideal to convert feelings of inferiority to superiority (or rather completeness). The desires of the self ideal were countered by social and ethical demands.
Beck	Beck was initially trained as a psychoanalyst and conducted research on the psychoanalytic treatment of depression. With out the strong ability to collect data to this end, he began exploring cognitive approaches to treatment and originated cognitive behavior therapy.
Apperception	A newly experienced sensation is related to past experiences to form an understood situation. For Wundt, consciousness is composed of two "stages:" There is a large capacity working memory called the Blickfeld and the narrower consciousness called Apperception, or selective attention.
Thematic Apperception Test	The Thematic Apperception Test uses a standard series of provocative yet ambiguous pictures about which the subject must tell a story. Each story is carefully analyzed to uncover underlying needs, attitudes, and patterns of reaction.
Ego	In Freud's view the Ego serves to balance our primitive needs and our moral beliefs and taboos. Relying on experience, a healthy Ego provides the ability to adapt to reality and interact with the outside world.
Psychometric	Psychometric study is concerned with the theory and technique of psychological measurement, which includes the measurement of knowledge, abilities, attitudes, and personality traits. The field is primarily concerned with the study of differences between individuals
American Psychological Association	The American Psychological Association is a professional organization representing psychology in the US. The mission statement is to "advance psychology as a science and profession and as a means of promoting health, education , and human welfare".
Testimonial	A testimonial or endorsement is a written or spoken statement, sometimes from a public figure, sometimes from a private citizen, extolling the virtue of some product, which is used in the promotion and advertising of that product.
Survey	A method of scientific investigation in which a large sample of people answer questions about their attitudes or behavior is referred to as a survey.
Generalization	In conditioning, the tendency for a conditioned response to be evoked by stimuli that are similar to the stimulus to which the response was conditioned is a generalization. The greater the similarity among the stimuli, the greater the probability of generalization.
Trauma	Trauma refers to a severe physical injury or wound to the body caused by an external force, or a psychological shock having a lasting effect on mental life.
Rotter	Rotter focused on the application of social learning theory (SLT) to clinical psychology. She introduced the ideas of learning from generalized expectancies of reinforcement and internal/ external locus of control (self-initiated change versus change influenced by others).

	According to Rotter, health outcomes could be improved by the development of a sense of personal control over one's life.
Quantitative	A quantitative property is one that exists in a range of magnitudes, and can therefore be measured. Measurements of any particular quantitative property are expressed as as a specific quantity, referred to as a unit, multiplied by a number.
Psychiatrist	A psychiatrist is a physician who specializes in the diagnosis and treatment of psychological disorders.
Object relation	Object relation theory is the idea that the ego-self exists only in relation to other objects, which may be external or internal.
Need for achievement	Need for Achievement is a term introduced by David McClelland into the field of psychology, referring to an individual's desire for significant accomplishment, mastering of skills, control, or high standards.
Psychodynamic	Most psychodynamic approaches are centered around the idea of a maladapted function developed early in life (usually childhood) which are at least in part unconscious. This maladapted function (a.k.a. defense mechanism) does not do well in place of a normal/healthy one.
Correlation	A statistical technique for determining the degree of association between two or more variables is referred to as correlation.
Illusory correlation	Illusory correlation is the phenomenon of seeing the relationship one expects in a set of data even when no such relationship exists.
Homosexuality	Homosexuality refers to a sexual orientation characterized by aesthetic attraction, romantic love, and sexual desire exclusively for members of the same sex or gender identity.
Mental retardation	Mental retardation refers to having significantly below-average intellectual functioning and limitations in at least two areas of adaptive functioning. Many categorize retardation as mild, moderate, severe, or profound.
Thought disorder	Thought disorder describes a persistent underlying disturbance to conscious thought and is classified largely by its effects on speech and writing. Affected persons may show pressure of speech, derailment or flight of ideas, thought blocking, rhyming, punning, or word salad.
Affect	A subjective feeling or emotional tone often accompanied by bodily expressions noticeable to others is called affect.
Informed consent	The term used by psychologists to indicate that a person has agreed to participate in research after receiving information about the purposes of the study and the nature of the treatments is informed consent. Even with informed consent, subjects may withdraw from any experiment at any time.
Obedience	Obedience is the willingness to follow the will of others. Humans have been shown to be surprisingly obedient in the presence of perceived legitimate authority figures, as demonstrated by the Milgram experiment in the 1960s.
Psychological test	Psychological test refers to a standardized measure of a sample of a person's behavior.
Discrimination	In Learning theory, discrimination refers the ability to distinguish between a conditioned stimulus and other stimuli. It can be brought about by extensive training or differential reinforcement. In social terms, it is the denial of privileges to a person or a group on the basis of prejudice.
Motivation	In psychology, motivation is the driving force (desire) behind all actions of an organism.
IQ test	An IQ test is a standardized test developed to measure a person's cognitive abilities

	("intelligence") in relation to their age group.
Feedback	Feedback refers to information returned to a person about the effects a response has had.
Personality test	A personality test aims to describe aspects of a person's character that remain stable across situations.

Construct	A generalized concept, such as anxiety or gravity, is a construct.
Paranoia	In popular culture, the term paranoia is usually used to describe excessive concern about one's own well-being, sometimes suggesting a person holds persecutory beliefs concerning a threat to themselves or their property and is often linked to a belief in conspiracy theories.
Ego	In Freud's view the Ego serves to balance our primitive needs and our moral beliefs and taboos. Relying on experience, a healthy Ego provides the ability to adapt to reality and interact with the outside world.
Variable	A variable refers to a measurable factor, characteristic, or attribute of an individual or a system.
Personality	Personality refers to the pattern of enduring characteristics that differentiates a person, the patterns of behaviors that make each individual unique.
Behavioral assessment	Direct measures of an individual's behavior used to describe characteristics indicative of personality are called behavioral assessment.
Irrelevant questions	In a polygraph exam, neutral, non-threatening, or non-emotional questions are referred to as irrelevant questions.
Inference	Inference is the act or process of drawing a conclusion based solely on what one already knows.
Insight	Insight refers to a sudden awareness of the relationships among various elements that had previously appeared to be independent of one another.
Skinner	Skinner conducted research on shaping behavior through positive and negative reinforcement, and demonstrated operant conditioning, a technique which he developed in contrast with classical conditioning.
Functional analysis	A systematic study of behavior in which one identifies the stimuli that trigger the behavior and the reinforcers that maintain it is a functional analysis. Relations between the two become the cause-and-effect relationships in behavior and are the laws of a science. A synthesis of these various laws expressed in quantitative terms yields a comprehensive picture of the organism as a behaving system without postulating internal processes.
Stimulus	A change in an environmental condition that elicits a response is a stimulus.
Reinforcement	In operant conditioning, reinforcement is any change in an environment that (a) occurs after the behavior, (b) seems to make that behavior re-occur more often in the future and (c) that reoccurence of behavior must be the result of the change.
Clinician	A health professional authorized to provide services to people suffering from one or more pathologies is a clinician.
Antecedent condition	The event that precedes another event is called the antecedent condition.
Attention	Attention is the cognitive process of selectively concentrating on one thing while ignoring other things. Psychologists have labeled three types of attention: sustained attention, selective attention, and divided attention.
SORC	SORC refers to the four sets of variables that are the focus of behavioral assessment: situational determinants, organismic variables, responses, and reinforcement contingencies.
Reflection	Reflection is the process of rephrasing or repeating thoughts and feelings expressed, making the person more aware of what they are saying or thinking.
Trait	An enduring personality characteristic that tends to lead to certain behaviors is called a

	trait. The term trait also means a genetically inherited feature of an organism.
Baseline	Measure of a particular behavior or process taken before the introduction of the independent variable or treatment is called the baseline.
Etiology	Etiology is the study of causation. The term is used in philosophy, physics and biology in reference to the causes of various phenomena. It is generally the study of why things occur, or even the reasons behind the way that things act.
Idiographic	An idiographic investigation studies the characteristics of an individual in depth.
Maladaptive	In psychology, a behavior or trait is adaptive when it helps an individual adjust and function well within their social environment. A maladaptive behavior or trait is counterproductive to the individual.
Stages	Stages represent relatively discrete periods of time in which functioning is qualitatively different from functioning at other periods.
Motivation	In psychology, motivation is the driving force (desire) behind all actions of an organism.
Feedback	Feedback refers to information returned to a person about the effects a response has had.
Behavior therapy	Behavior therapy refers to the systematic application of the principles of learning to direct modification of a client's problem behaviors.
Presenting problem	The presenting problem is the original complaint reported by the client to the therapist. The actual treated problem may sometimes be a modification derived from the presenting problem or entirely different..
Psychological test	Psychological test refers to a standardized measure of a sample of a person's behavior.
Health psychology	The field of psychology that studies the relationships between psychological factors and the prevention and treatment of physical illness is called health psychology.
Clinical psychology	Clinical psychology is involved in the diagnosis, assessment, and treatment of patients with mental or behavioral disorders, and conducts research in these various areas.
Learning	Learning is a relatively permanent change in behavior that results from experience. Thus, to attribute a behavioral change to learning, the change must be relatively permanent and must result from experience.
Learning disability	A learning disability exists when there is a significant discrepancy between one's ability and achievement.
Psychopathology	Psychopathology refers to the field concerned with the nature and development of mental disorders.
Chronic	Chronic refers to a relatively long duration, usually more than a few months.
Clinical assessment	A clinical assessment is a systematic evaluation and measurement of psychological, biological, and social factors in a person presenting with a possible psychological disorder.
Individual differences	Individual differences psychology studies the ways in which individual people differ in their behavior. This is distinguished from other aspects of psychology in that although psychology is ostensibly a study of individuals, modern psychologists invariably study groups.
Questionnaire	A self-report method of data collection or clinical assessment method in which the individual being studied checks off items on a printed list, answers multiple-choice questions, or writes out answers to essay questions aimed at producing a selfdescription is called questionnaire.
Social skills	Social skills are skills used to interact and communicate with others to assist status in the

	social structure and other motivations.
Mental disorder	Mental disorder refers to a disturbance in a person's emotions, drives, thought processes, or behavior that involves serious and relatively prolonged distress and/or impairment in ability to function, is not simply a normal response to some event or set of events in the person's environment.
Naturalistic observation	Naturalistic observation is a method of observation that involves observing subjects in their natural habitats. Researchers take great care in avoiding making interferences with the behavior they are observing by using unobtrusive methods.
Phobia	A persistent, irrational fear of an object, situation, or activity that the person feels compelled to avoid is referred to as a phobia.
Direct observation	Direct observation refers to assessing behavior through direct surveillance.
Clinical psychologist	A psychologist, usually with a Ph.D, whose training is in the diagnosis, treatment, or research of psychological and behavioral disorders is a clinical psychologist.
Projective test	A projective test is a personality test designed to let a person respond to ambiguous stimuli, presumably revealing hidden emotions and internal conflicts. This is different from an "objective test" in which responses are analyzed according to a universal standard rather than an individual psychiatrist's judgement.
Coding	In senation, coding is the process by which information about the quality and quantity of a stimulus is preserved in the pattern of action potentials sent through sensory neurons to the central nervous system.
Reid	Reid was the founder of the Scottish School of Common Sense, and played an integral role in the Scottish Enlightenment. He advocated direct realism, or common sense realism, and argued strongly against the Theory of Ideas advocated by John Locke and René Descartes.
Mental retardation	Mental retardation refers to having significantly below-average intellectual functioning and limitations in at least two areas of adaptive functioning. Many categorize retardation as mild, moderate, severe, or profound.
Reliability	Reliability means the extent to which a test produces a consistent , reproducible score .
Social learning	Social learning is learning that occurs as a function of observing, retaining and replicating behavior observed in others. Although social learning can occur at any stage in life, it is thought to be particularly important during childhood, particularly as authority becomes important.
Antipsychotic	The term antipsychotic is applied to a group of drugs used to treat psychosis.
Clozapine	Clozapine (trade names Clozaril), was the first of the atypical antipsychotic drugs. Clozapine is the only FDA-approved medication indicated for treatment-resistant schizophrenia and for reducing the risk of suicidal behavior in patients with schizophrenia.
Behavioral observation	A form of behavioral assessment that entails careful observation of a person's overt behavior in a particular situation is behavioral observation.
Habit	A habit is a response that has become completely separated from its eliciting stimulus. Early learning theorists used the term to describe S-R associations, however not all S-R associations become a habit, rather many are extinguished after reinforcement is withdrawn.
Bandura	Bandura is best known for his work on social learning theory or Social Cognitivism. His famous Bobo doll experiment illustrated that people learn from observing others.
Demand	Demand characteristics suggest to the subjects what the researcher expects from it's

characteristics	participants.
Attitude	An enduring mental representation of a person, place, or thing that evokes an emotional response and related behavior is called attitude.
Psychophysio-ogical assessment	Psychophysiological assessment refers to measurement of changes in the nervous system that correspond to psychological or emotional events such as anxiety, stress, and sexual arousal.
Nervous system	The body's electrochemical communication circuitry, made up of billions of neurons is a nervous system.
Schizophrenia	Schizophrenia is characterized by persistent defects in the perception or expression of reality. A person suffering from untreated schizophrenia typically demonstrates grossly disorganized thinking, and may also experience delusions or auditory hallucinations
Anxiety	Anxiety is a complex combination of the feeling of fear, apprehension and worry often accompanied by physical sensations such as palpitations, chest pain and/or shortness of breath.
Autonomic nervous system	A division of the peripheral nervous system, the autonomic nervous system, regulates glands and activities such as heartbeat, respiration, digestion, and dilation of the pupils. It is responsible for homeostasis, maintaining a relatively constant internal environment .
Central nervous system	The vertebrate central nervous system consists of the brain and spinal cord.
Emotion	An emotion is a mental states that arise spontaneously, rather than through conscious effort. They are often accompanied by physiological changes.
Affect	A subjective feeling or emotional tone often accompanied by bodily expressions noticeable to others is called affect.
Depression	In everyday language depression refers to any downturn in mood, which may be relatively transitory and perhaps due to something trivial. This is differentiated from Clinical depression which is marked by symptoms that last two weeks or more and are so severe that they interfere with daily living.
Validity	The extent to which a test measures what it is intended to measure is called validity.
Rorschach	The Rorschach inkblot test is a method of psychological evaluation. It is a projective test associated with the Freudian school of thought. Psychologists use this test to try to probe the unconscious minds of their patients.
Schema	Schema refers to a way of mentally representing the world, such as a belief or an expectation, that can influence perception of persons, objects, and situations.
Content validity	The degree to which the content of a test is representative of the domain it's supposed to cover is referred to as its content validity.
A priori	The term A Priori is considered to mean propositional knowledge that can be had without, or "prior to", experience.
Construct validity	The extent to which there is evidence that a test measures a particular hypothetical construct is referred to as construct validity.
Bias	A bias is a prejudice in a general or specific sense, usually in the sense for having a preference to one particular point of view or ideological perspective.
Halo effect	The halo effect occurs when a person's positive or negative traits seem to "spill over" from one area of their personality to another in others' perceptions of them.

Sexual dysfunction	Sexual dysfunction is difficulty during any stage of the sexual act (which includes desire, arousal, orgasm, and resolution) that prevents the individual or couple from enjoying sexual activity.
Representative sample	Representative sample refers to a sample of participants selected from the larger population in such a way that important subgroups within the population are included in the sample in the same proportions as they are found in the larger population.
Acquisition	Acquisition is the process of adapting to the environment, learning or becoming conditioned. In classical conditoning terms, it is the initial learning of the stimulus response link, which involves a neutral stimulus being associated with a unconditioned stimulus and becoming a conditioned stimulus.
Research design	A research design tests a hypothesis. The basic typess are: descriptive, correlational, and experimental.
Rotter	Rotter focused on the application of social learning theory (SLT) to clinical psychology. She introduced the ideas of learning from generalized expectancies of reinforcement and internal/ external locus of control (self-initiated change versus change influenced by others). According to Rotter, health outcomes could be improved by the development of a sense of personal control over one's life.
Assertiveness	Assertiveness basically means the ability to express your thoughts and feelings in a way that clearly states your needs and keeps the lines of communication open with the other.
Assertiveness training	In behavior therapy, a direct method of training people to express their own desires and feelings and to maintain their own rights in interactions with others, while at the same time respecting the others' rights is called assertiveness training.
Behavioral rehearsal	Behavior therapy technique in which the client practices coping with troublesome or anxiety arousing situations in a safe and supervised situation is a behavioral rehearsal.
Perception	Perception is the process of acquiring, interpreting, selecting, and organizing sensory information.
Survey	A method of scientific investigation in which a large sample of people answer questions about their attitudes or behavior is referred to as a survey.
Cognition	The intellectual processes through which information is obtained, transformed, stored, retrieved, and otherwise used is cognition.
Task analysis	The procedure of identifying the component elements of a behavior chain is called task analysis.
Shyness	A tendency to avoid others plus uneasiness and strain when socializing is called shyness.
Cognitive therapy	Cognitive therapy is a kind of psychotherapy used to treat depression, anxiety disorders, phobias, and other forms of mental disorder. It involves recognizing distorted thinking and learning how to replace it with more realistic thoughts and actions.
Attributional style	One's tendency to attribute one's behavior to internal or external factors, stable or unstable factors, and so on is their attributional style.
Social phobia	An irrational, excessive fear of public scrutiny is referred to as social phobia.
Population	Population refers to all members of a well-defined group of organisms, events, or things.
Diagnostic and Statistical Manual of Mental	The Diagnostic and Statistical Manual of Mental Disorders, published by the American Psychiatric Association, is the handbook used most often in diagnosing mental disorders in the United States and internationally.

Disorders	
Predictive validity	Predictive validity refers to the relation between test scores and the student 's future performance .
Ecological momentary assessment	Ecological momentary assessment is a form of self-observation and the collecting of data in real time.

Clinician	A health professional authorized to provide services to people suffering from one or more pathologies is a clinician.
Psychological test	Psychological test refers to a standardized measure of a sample of a person's behavior.
Cognitive structure	According to Piaget, the number of schemata available to an organism at any given time constitutes that organism's cognitive structure. How the organism interacts with its environment depends on the current cognitive structure available. As the cognitive structure develops, new assimilations can occur.
Psychodynamic	Most psychodynamic approaches are centered around the idea of a maladapted function developed early in life (usually childhood) which are at least in part unconscious. This maladapted function (a.k.a. defense mechanism) does not do well in place of a normal/healthy one.
Inference	Inference is the act or process of drawing a conclusion based solely on what one already knows.
Population	Population refers to all members of a well-defined group of organisms, events, or things.
Generalization	In conditioning, the tendency for a conditioned response to be evoked by stimuli that are similar to the stimulus to which the response was conditioned is a generalization. The greater the similarity among the stimuli, the greater the probability of generalization.
Deduction	Deduction refers to reasoning from the general to the particular, as in the case of creating an expected hypothesis for a particular experiment from a general theoretical statement.
Empirical	Empirical means the use of working hypotheses which are capable of being disproved using observation or experiment.
Standardized test	An oral or written assessment for which an individual receives a score indicating how the individual reponded relative to a previously tested large sample of others is referred to as a standardized test.
Regression	Return to a form of behavior characteristic of an earlier stage of development is called regression.
Norms	In testing, standards of test performance that permit the comparison of one person's score on the test to the scores of others who have taken the same test are referred to as norms.
Regression equation	A regression equation refers to a mathematical relationship where one variable is predictable from another.
Psychometric	Psychometric study is concerned with the theory and technique of psychological measurement, which includes the measurement of knowledge, abilities, attitudes, and personality traits. The field is primarily concerned with the study of differences between individuals
Projective test	A projective test is a personality test designed to let a person respond to ambiguous stimuli, presumably revealing hidden emotions and internal conflicts. This is different from an "objective test" in which responses are analyzed according to a universal standard rather than an individual psychiatrist's judgement.
Normative	The term normative is used to describe the effects of those structures of culture which regulate the function of social activity.
Quantitative	A quantitative property is one that exists in a range of magnitudes, and can therefore be measured. Measurements of any particular quantitative property are expressed as as a specific quantity, referred to as a unit, multiplied by a number.
Hypothesis	A specific statement about behavior or mental processes that is testable through research is a hypothesis.

Correlation	A statistical technique for determining the degree of association between two or more variables is referred to as correlation.
Behavior therapy	Behavior therapy refers to the systematic application of the principles of learning to direct modification of a client's problem behaviors.
Psychoanalytic	Freud's theory that unconscious forces act as determinants of personality is called psychoanalytic theory. The theory is a developmental theory characterized by critical stages of development.
Variable	A variable refers to a measurable factor, characteristic, or attribute of an individual or a system.
Intuition	Quick, impulsive thought that does not make use of formal logic or clear reasoning is referred to as intuition.
Rorschach	The Rorschach inkblot test is a method of psychological evaluation. It is a projective test associated with the Freudian school of thought. Psychologists use this test to try to probe the unconscious minds of their patients.
Depression	In everyday language depression refers to any downturn in mood, which may be relatively transitory and perhaps due to something trivial. This is differentiated from Clinical depression which is marked by symptoms that last two weeks or more and are so severe that they interfere with daily living.
Attention	Attention is the cognitive process of selectively concentrating on one thing while ignoring other things. Psychologists have labeled three types of attention: sustained attention, selective attention, and divided attention.
Clinical psychologist	A psychologist, usually with a Ph.D, whose training is in the diagnosis, treatment, or research of psychological and behavioral disorders is a clinical psychologist.
Personality	Personality refers to the pattern of enduring characteristics that differentiates a person, the patterns of behaviors that make each individual unique.
Barnum effect	The Forer effect, or Barnum effect, is the observation that individuals will give high accuracy ratings to descriptions of their personality that supposedly are tailored specifically for them, but are in fact vague and general enough to apply to a wide range of people.
Alcoholic	An alcoholic is dependent on alcohol as characterized by craving, loss of control, physical dependence and withdrawal symptoms, and tolerance.
Personality inventory	A self-report questionnaire by which an examinee indicates whether statements assessing habitual tendencies apply to him or her is referred to as a personality inventory.
Prognosis	A forecast about the probable course of an illess is referred to as prognosis.
Heterogeneous	A heterogeneous compound, mixture, or other such object is one that consists of many different items, which are often not easily sorted or separated, though they are clearly distinct.
Clinical psychology	Clinical psychology is involved in the diagnosis, assessment, and treatment of patients with mental or behavioral disorders, and conducts research in these various areas.
Suicide	Suicide behavior is rare in childhood but escalates in adolescence. The suicide rate increases in a linear fashion from adolescence through late adulthood.
Counselor	A counselor is a mental health professional who specializes in helping people with problems not involving serious mental disorders.
Aptitude test	A test designed to predict a person's ability in a particular area or line of work is called

	an aptitude test.
Survey	A method of scientific investigation in which a large sample of people answer questions about their attitudes or behavior is referred to as a survey.
Clinical method	Studying psychological problems and therapies in clinical settings is referred to as the clinical method. It usually involves case histories, pathology, or non-experimentally controlled environments.
Algorithm	A systematic procedure for solving a problem that works invariably when it is correctly applied is called an algorithm.
Psychosis	Psychosis is a generic term for mental states in which the components of rational thought and perception are severely impaired. Persons experiencing a psychosis may experience hallucinations, hold paranoid or delusional beliefs, demonstrate personality changes and exhibit disorganized thinking. This is usually accompanied by features such as a lack of insight into the unusual or bizarre nature of their behavior, difficulties with social interaction and impairments in carrying out the activities of daily living.
Neurosis	Neurosis, any mental disorder that, although may cause distress, does not interfere with rational thought or the persons' ability to function.
Psychotherapy	Psychotherapy is a set of techniques based on psychological principles intended to improve mental health, emotional or behavioral issues.
Liver	The liver plays a major role in metabolism and has a number of functions in the body including detoxification, glycogen storage and plasma protein synthesis. It also produces bile, which is important for digestion. The liver converts most carbohydrates, proteing, and fats into glucose.
Bias	A bias is a prejudice in a general or specific sense, usually in the sense for having a preference to one particular point of view or ideological perspective.
Major depression	Major depression is characterized by a severely depressed mood that persists for at least two weeks. Episodes of depression may start suddenly or slowly and can occur several times through a person's life. The disorder may be categorized as "single episode" or "recurrent" depending on whether previous episodes have been experienced before.
Empirical evidence	Facts or information based on direct observation or experience are referred to as empirical evidence.
Social class	Social class describes the relationships between people in hierarchical societies or cultures. Those with more power usually subordinate those with less power.
Antipsychotic	The term antipsychotic is applied to a group of drugs used to treat psychosis.
Wisdom	Wisdom is the ability to make correct judgments and decisions. It is an intangible quality gained through experience. Whether or not something is wise is determined in a pragmatic sense by its popularity, how long it has been around, and its ability to predict against future events.
Society	The social sciences use the term society to mean a group of people that form a semi-closed (or semi-open) social system, in which most interactions are with other individuals belonging to the group.
Personality trait	According to the Diagnostic and Statistical Manual of the American Psychiatric Association, a personality trait is a "prominent aspect of personality that is exhibited in a wide range of important social and personal contexts. ...".
Trait	An enduring personality characteristic that tends to lead to certain behaviors is called a trait. The term trait also means a genetically inherited feature of an organism.

Defense mechanism	A Defense mechanism is a set of unconscious ways to protect one's personality from unpleasant thoughts and realities which may otherwise cause anxiety. The notion is an integral part of the psychoanalytic theory.
Information processing	Information processing is an approach to the goal of understanding human thinking. The essence of the approach is to see cognition as being essentially computational in nature, with mind being the software and the brain being the hardware.
Syndrome	The term syndrome is the association of several clinically recognizable features, signs, symptoms, phenomena or characteristics which often occur together, so that the presence of one feature indicates the presence of the others.
Psychopathology	Psychopathology refers to the field concerned with the nature and development of mental disorders.
Pathology	Pathology is the study of the processes underlying disease and other forms of illness, harmful abnormality, or dysfunction.
Personality test	A personality test aims to describe aspects of a person's character that remain stable across situations.
Behavioral assessment	Direct measures of an individual's behavior used to describe characteristics indicative of personality are called behavioral assessment.
Mischel	Mischel is known for his cognitive social learning model of personality that focuses on the specific cognitive variables that mediate the manner in which new experiences affect the individual.
Reliability	Reliability means the extent to which a test produces a consistent , reproducible score .
Validity	The extent to which a test measures what it is intended to measure is called validity.
Test battery	A group of tests and interviews given to the same individual is a test battery.
Homosexuality	Homosexuality refers to a sexual orientation characterized by aesthetic attraction, romantic love, and sexual desire exclusively for members of the same sex or gender identity.
Socioeconomic	Socioeconomic pertains to the study of the social and economic impacts of any product or service offering, market intervention or other activity on an economy as a whole and on the companies, organization and individuals who are its main economic actors.
Socioeconomic Status	A family's socioeconomic status is based on family income, parental education level, parental occupation, and social status in the community. Those with high status often have more success in preparing their children for school because they have access to a wide range of resources.
Insight therapy	Insight therapy encourages self-awareness. They include the psychodynamic and humanistic therapies.
Insight	Insight refers to a sudden awareness of the relationships among various elements that had previously appeared to be independent of one another.
Schizophrenia	Schizophrenia is characterized by persistent defects in the perception or expression of reality. A person suffering from untreated schizophrenia typically demonstrates grossly disorganized thinking, and may also experience delusions or auditory hallucinations
Paranoid	The term paranoid is typically used in a general sense to signify any self-referential delusion, or more specifically, to signify a delusion involving the fear of persecution.
Paranoid schizophrenia	Paranoid schizophrenia is a type of schizophrenia characterized primarily by delusions-commonly of persecution-and by vivid hallucinations .

Affect | A subjective feeling or emotional tone often accompanied by bodily expressions noticeable to others is called affect.

Psychiatrist | A psychiatrist is a physician who specializes in the diagnosis and treatment of psychological disorders.

Feedback | Feedback refers to information returned to a person about the effects a response has had.

Mental retardation | Mental retardation refers to having significantly below-average intellectual functioning and limitations in at least two areas of adaptive functioning. Many categorize retardation as mild, moderate, severe, or profound.

Guilford | Guilford observed that most individuals display a preference for either convergent or divergent thinking. Scientists and engineers typically prefer the former and artists and performers, the latter.

Learning | Learning is a relatively permanent change in behavior that results from experience. Thus, to attribute a behavioral change to learning, the change must be relatively permanent and must result from experience.

Behavioral observation | A form of behavioral assessment that entails careful observation of a person's overt behavior in a particular situation is behavioral observation.

Narcotic | The term narcotic originally referred to a variety of substances that induced sleep (such state is narcosis). In legal context, narcotic refers to opium, opium derivatives, and their semisynthetic or totally synthetic substitutes.

Minnesota Multiphasic Personality Inventory | The Minnesota Multiphasic Personality Inventory is the most frequently used test in the mental health fields. This assessment or test helps identify personal, social, and behavioral problems in psychiatric patients. This test helps provide relevant information to aid in problem identification, diagnosis, and treatment planning for the patient.

Nightmare | Nightmare was the original term for the state later known as waking dream, and more currently as sleep paralysis, associated with rapid eye movement (REM) periods of sleep.

Arousal | Arousal is a physiological and psychological state involving the activation of the reticular activating system in the brain stem, the autonomic nervous system and the endocrine system, leading to increased heart rate and blood pressure and a condition of alertness and readiness to respond.

Premorbid | Premorbid refers to individual's level of functioning prior to the development of a disorder.

Denial | Denial is a psychological defense mechanism in which a person faced with a fact that is uncomfortable or painful to accept rejects it instead, insisting that it is not true despite what may be overwhelming evidence.

Reality testing | Reality testing is the capacity to perceive one's environment and oneself according to accurate sensory impressions.

Thought disorder | Thought disorder describes a persistent underlying disturbance to conscious thought and is classified largely by its effects on speech and writing. Affected persons may show pressure of speech, derailment or flight of ideas, thought blocking, rhyming, punning, or word salad.

Emotion | An emotion is a mental states that arise spontaneously, rather than through conscious effort. They are often accompanied by physiological changes.

Acute | Acute means sudden, sharp, and abrupt. Usually short in duration.

Social phobia | An irrational, excessive fear of public scrutiny is referred to as social phobia.

Affective | Affective is the way people react emotionally, their ability to feel another living thing's pain or joy.

Phobia	A persistent, irrational fear of an object, situation, or activity that the person feels compelled to avoid is referred to as a phobia.
Stress disorder	A significant emotional disturbance caused by stresses outside the range of normal human experience is referred to as stress disorder.
Global Assessment of Functioning	Global Assessment of Functioning is a numeric scale (0 through 100) used by mental health clinicians and doctors to rate the social, occupational and psychological functioning of adults.
Construct	A generalized concept, such as anxiety or gravity, is a construct.
Structured interview	Structured interview refers to an interview in which the questions are set out in a prescribed fashion for the interviewer. It assists professionals in making diagnostic decisions based upon standardized criteria.
Illusory correlation	Illusory correlation is the phenomenon of seeing the relationship one expects in a set of data even when no such relationship exists.

Attention	Attention is the cognitive process of selectively concentrating on one thing while ignoring other things. Psychologists have labeled three types of attention: sustained attention, selective attention, and divided attention.
Psychotherapy	Psychotherapy is a set of techniques based on psychological principles intended to improve mental health, emotional or behavioral issues.
Personality	Personality refers to the pattern of enduring characteristics that differentiates a person, the patterns of behaviors that make each individual unique.
Elaboration	The extensiveness of processing at any given level of memory is called elaboration. The use of elaboration changes developmentally. Adolescents are more likely to use elaboration spontaneously than children.
Cognitive therapy	Cognitive therapy is a kind of psychotherapy used to treat depression, anxiety disorders, phobias, and other forms of mental disorder. It involves recognizing distorted thinking and learning how to replace it with more realistic thoughts and actions.
Gestalt therapy	Gestalt therapy is a form of psychotherapy, based on the experiential ideal of "here and now," and relationships with others and the world. By focusing the individual on their self-awareness as part of present reality, new insights can be made into their behavior, and they can engage in self-healing.
Psychoanalysis	Psychoanalysis refers to the school of psychology that emphasizes the importance of unconscious motives and conflicts as determinants of human behavior. It was Freud's method of exploring human personality.
Internal validity	Internal validity is a term pertaining to scientific research that signifies the extent to which the conditions within a research design were conducive to drawing the conclusions the researcher was interested in drawing.
Validity	The extent to which a test measures what it is intended to measure is called validity.
External validity	External validity is a term used in scientific research. It signifies the extent to which the results of a study can be applied to circumstances outside the specific setting in which the research was carried out. In other words, it addresses the question "Can this research be applied to 'the real world'?"
Random assignment	Assignment of participants to experimental and control groups by chance is called random assignment. Random assigment reduces the likelihood that the results are due to preexisiting systematic differences between the groups.
Control group	A group that does not receive the treatment effect in an experiment is referred to as the control group or sometimes as the comparison group.
Empirical evidence	Facts or information based on direct observation or experience are referred to as empirical evidence.
Empirical	Empirical means the use of working hypotheses which are capable of being disproved using observation or experiment.
Survey	A method of scientific investigation in which a large sample of people answer questions about their attitudes or behavior is referred to as a survey.
Median	The median is a number that separates the higher half of a sample, a population, or a probability distribution from the lower half. It is the middle value in a distribution, above and below which lie an equal number of values.
Depression	In everyday language depression refers to any downturn in mood, which may be relatively transitory and perhaps due to something trivial. This is differentiated from Clinical depression which is marked by symptoms that last two weeks or more and are so severe that

	they interfere with daily living.
Anxiety	Anxiety is a complex combination of the feeling of fear, apprehension and worry often accompanied by physical sensations such as palpitations, chest pain and/or shortness of breath.
Phobia	A persistent, irrational fear of an object, situation, or activity that the person feels compelled to avoid is referred to as a phobia.
Psychiatrist	A psychiatrist is a physician who specializes in the diagnosis and treatment of psychological disorders.
Specific phobia	A specific phobia is a generic term for anxiety disorders that amount to unreasonable or irrational fear or anxiety related with exposure to specific objects or situations. As a result, the affected persons tend to actively avoid these objects or situations.
Psychopathology	Psychopathology refers to the field concerned with the nature and development of mental disorders.
William James	Functionalism as a psychology developed out of Pragmatism as a philosophy: To find the meaning of an idea, you have to look at its consequences. This led William James and his students towards an emphasis on cause and effect, prediction and control, and observation of environment and behavior, over the careful introspection of the Structuralists.
Society	The social sciences use the term society to mean a group of people that form a semi-closed (or semi-open) social system, in which most interactions are with other individuals belonging to the group.
American Psychological Association	The American Psychological Association is a professional organization representing psychology in the US. The mission statement is to "advance psychology as a science and profession and as a means of promoting health, education , and human welfare".
Immune system	The most important function of the human immune system occurs at the cellular level of the blood and tissues. The lymphatic and blood circulation systems are highways for specialized white blood cells. These cells include B cells, T cells, natural killer cells, and macrophages. All function with the primary objective of recognizing, attacking and destroying bacteria, viruses, cancer cells, and all substances seen as foreign.
Assimilation	According to Piaget, assimilation is the process of the organism interacting with the environment given the organism's cognitive structure. Assimilation is reuse of schemas to fit new information.
Affective	Affective is the way people react emotionally, their ability to feel another living thing's pain or joy.
Catharsis	Catharsis has been adopted by modern psychotherapy as the act of giving expression to deep emotions often associated with events in the individuals past which have never before been adequately expressed.
Empathy	Empathy is the recognition and understanding of the states of mind, including beliefs, desires and particularly emotions of others without injecting your own.
Behavioral regulation	Adaptive behavior that help animals achieve a homeostatic state is called behavioral regulation.
Positive relationship	Statistically, a positive relationship refers to a mathematical relationship in which increases in one measure are matched by increases in the other.
Therapeutic alliance	A therapeutic alliance refers to a caring relationship that unites a therapist and a client in working to solve the client's problems.

Wisdom	Wisdom is the ability to make correct judgments and decisions. It is an intangible quality gained through experience. Whether or not something is wise is determined in a pragmatic sense by its popularity, how long it has been around, and its ability to predict against future events.
Authoritarian	The term authoritarian is used to describe a style that enforces strong and sometimes oppressive measures against those in its sphere of influence, generally without attempts at gaining their consent.
Scheme	According to Piaget, a hypothetical mental structure that permits the classification and organization of new information is called a scheme.
Emotion	An emotion is a mental states that arise spontaneously, rather than through conscious effort. They are often accompanied by physiological changes.
Habituation	In habituation there is a progressive reduction in the response probability with continued repetition of a stimulus.
Insight	Insight refers to a sudden awareness of the relationships among various elements that had previously appeared to be independent of one another.
Learning	Learning is a relatively permanent change in behavior that results from experience. Thus, to attribute a behavioral change to learning, the change must be relatively permanent and must result from experience.
Bandura	Bandura is best known for his work on social learning theory or Social Cognitivism. His famous Bobo doll experiment illustrated that people learn from observing others.
Placebo effect	The placebo effect is the phenomenon that a patient's symptoms can be alleviated by an otherwise ineffective treatment, apparently because the individual expects or believes that it will work.
Placebo	Placebo refers to a bogus treatment that has the appearance of being genuine.
Variable	A variable refers to a measurable factor, characteristic, or attribute of an individual or a system.
Motivation	In psychology, motivation is the driving force (desire) behind all actions of an organism.
Affect	A subjective feeling or emotional tone often accompanied by bodily expressions noticeable to others is called affect.
Generalization	In conditioning, the tendency for a conditioned response to be evoked by stimuli that are similar to the stimulus to which the response was conditioned is a generalization. The greater the similarity among the stimuli, the greater the probability of generalization.
Clinician	A health professional authorized to provide services to people suffering from one or more pathologies is a clinician.
Personality disorder	A mental disorder characterized by a set of inflexible, maladaptive personality traits that keep a person from functioning properly in society is referred to as a personality disorder.
Mental retardation	Mental retardation refers to having significantly below-average intellectual functioning and limitations in at least two areas of adaptive functioning. Many categorize retardation as mild, moderate, severe, or profound.
Behavior modification	Behavior Modification is a technique of altering an individual's reactions to stimuli through positive reinforcement and the extinction of maladaptive behavior.
Population	Population refers to all members of a well-defined group of organisms, events, or things.
Cognition	The intellectual processes through which information is obtained, transformed, stored,

retrieved, and otherwise used is cognition.

Psychodynamic | Most psychodynamic approaches are centered around the idea of a maladapted function developed early in life (usually childhood) which are at least in part unconscious. This maladapted function (a.k.a. defense mechanism) does not do well in place of a normal/healthy one.

Marijuana | Marijuana is the dried vegetable matter of the Cannabis sativa plant. It contains large concentrations of compounds that have medicinal and psychoactive effects when consumed, usually by smoking or eating.

Necessary condition | A circumstance required for a particular phenomenon to occur is a necessary condition if and only if the condition does not occur in the absense of the circumstance.

Prognosis | A forecast about the probable course of an illess is referred to as prognosis.

Acculturation | Acculturation is the obtainment of culture by an individual or a group of people.

Socioeconomic | Socioeconomic pertains to the study of the social and economic impacts of any product or service offering, market intervention or other activity on an economy as a whole and on the companies, organization and individuals who are its main economic actors.

Social class | Social class describes the relationships between people in hierarchical societies or cultures. Those with more power usually subordinate those with less power.

Presenting problem | The presenting problem is the original complaint reported by the client to the therapist. The actual treated problem may sometimes be a modification derived from the presenting problem or entirely different..

Clinical psychology | Clinical psychology is involved in the diagnosis, assessment, and treatment of patients with mental or behavioral disorders, and conducts research in these various areas.

Psychoanalyst | A psychoanalyst is a specially trained therapist who attempts to treat the individual by uncovering and revealing to the individual otherwise subconscious factors that are contributing to some undesirable behavor.

Ethnicity | Ethnicity refers to a characteristic based on cultural heritage, nationality characteristics, race, religion, and language.

Sympathetic | The sympathetic nervous system activates what is often termed the "fight or flight response". It is an automatic regulation system, that is, one that operates without the intervention of conscious thought.

Prejudice | Prejudice in general, implies coming to a judgment on the subject before learning where the preponderance of the evidence actually lies, or formation of a judgement without direct experience.

Trait | An enduring personality characteristic that tends to lead to certain behaviors is called a trait. The term trait also means a genetically inherited feature of an organism.

Personality trait | According to the Diagnostic and Statistical Manual of the American Psychiatric Association, a personality trait is a "prominent aspect of personality that is exhibited in a wide range of important social and personal contexts. ...".

Carl Rogers | Carl Rogers was instrumental in the development of non-directive psychotherapy, also known as "client-centered" psychotherapy. Rogers' basic tenets were unconditional positive regard, genuineness, and empathic understanding, with each demonstrated by the counselor.

Sufficient condition | To say that A is a sufficient condition for B is to say precisely the converse: that A cannot occur without B, or whenever A occurs, B occurs. That there is a fire is sufficient for there being smoke.

Behavior therapy | Behavior therapy refers to the systematic application of the principles of learning to direct

	modification of a client's problem behaviors.
Paraprofessional	A paraprofessional is an individual lacking a doctoral degree but trained to perform certain functions usually reserved for clinicians.
Informed consent	The term used by psychologists to indicate that a person has agreed to participate in research after receiving information about the purposes of the study and the nature of the treatments is informed consent. Even with informed consent, subjects may withdraw from any experiment at any time.
Psychoanalytic	Freud's theory that unconscious forces act as determinants of personality is called psychoanalytic theory. The theory is a developmental theory characterized by critical stages of development.
Stages	Stages represent relatively discrete periods of time in which functioning is qualitatively different from functioning at other periods.
Maladaptive	In psychology, a behavior or trait is adaptive when it helps an individual adjust and function well within their social environment. A maladaptive behavior or trait is counterproductive to the individual.
Attitude	An enduring mental representation of a person, place, or thing that evokes an emotional response and related behavior is called attitude.
Experimental group	Experimental group refers to any group receiving a treatment effect in an experiment.
Analog study	An investigation that attempts to replicate or simulate, under controlled conditions, a situation that occurs in real life is an analog study.
Psychological test	Psychological test refers to a standardized measure of a sample of a person's behavior.
Effect size	An effect size is the strength or magnitude of the difference between two sets of data or, in outcome studies, between two time points for the same population. (The degree to which the null hypothesis is false).
Standard deviation	In probability and statistics, the standard deviation is the most commonly used measure of statistical dispersion. Simply put, it measures how spread out the values in a data set are.
Alcoholism	A disorder that involves long-term, repeated, uncontrolled, compulsive, and excessive use of alcoholic beverages and that impairs the drinker's health and work and social relationships is called alcoholism.
Process research	Research on the mechanisms by which a therapy may bring improvement is called process research.
Behavioral therapy	The treatment of a mental disorder through the application of basic principles of conditioning and learning is called behavioral therapy.
Major depression	Major depression is characterized by a severely depressed mood that persists for at least two weeks. Episodes of depression may start suddenly or slowly and can occur several times through a person's life. The disorder may be categorized as "single episode" or "recurrent" depending on whether previous episodes have been experienced before.
Panic disorder	A panic attack is a period of intense fear or discomfort, typically with an abrupt onset and usually lasting no more than thirty minutes. The disorder is strikingly different from other types of anxiety, in that panic attacks are very sudden, appear to be unprovoked, and are often disabling. People who have repeated attacks, or feel severe anxiety about having another attack are said to have panic disorder.

Agoraphobia	An irrational fear of open, crowded places is called agoraphobia. Many people suffering from agoraphobia, however, are not afraid of the open spaces themselves, but of situations often associated with these spaces, such as social gatherings.
Lewin	Lewin ranks as one of the pioneers of social psychology, as one of the founders of group dynamics and as one of the most eminent representatives of Gestalt psychology.
Panic disorder with agoraphobia	In panic disorder with agoraphobia the person may experience severe panic attacks during situations where they feel trapped, insecure, out of control, or too far from their personal comfort zone. During severe bouts of anxiety, the person is confined not only to their home, but to one or two rooms and they may even become bedbound until their over-stimulated nervous system can quiet down, and their adrenaline levels return to a more normal level.
Clinical psychologist	A psychologist, usually with a Ph.D, whose training is in the diagnosis, treatment, or research of psychological and behavioral disorders is a clinical psychologist.
Rate of learning	The rate of learning is the change in responding due to the presence of a stimulus, over time.
Psychological testing	Psychological testing is a field characterized by the use of small samples of behavior in order to infer larger generalizations about a given individual. The technical term for psychological testing is psychometrics.
Life satisfaction	A person's attitudes about his or her overall life are referred to as life satisfaction.

Psychoanalytic	Freud's theory that unconscious forces act as determinants of personality is called psychoanalytic theory. The theory is a developmental theory characterized by critical stages of development.
Sigmund Freud	Sigmund Freud was the founder of the psychoanalytic school, based on his theory that unconscious motives control much behavior, that particular kinds of unconscious thoughts and memories are the source of neurosis, and that neurosis could be treated through bringing these unconscious thoughts and memories to consciousness in psychoanalytic treatment.
Personality	Personality refers to the pattern of enduring characteristics that differentiates a person, the patterns of behaviors that make each individual unique.
Psychoanalytic theory	Psychoanalytic theory is a general term for approaches to psychoanalysis which attempt to provide a conceptual framework more-or-less independent of clinical practice rather than based on empirical analysis of clinical cases.
Psychoanalysis	Psychoanalysis refers to the school of psychology that emphasizes the importance of unconscious motives and conflicts as determinants of human behavior. It was Freud's method of exploring human personality.
Clinical psychologist	A psychologist, usually with a Ph.D, whose training is in the diagnosis, treatment, or research of psychological and behavioral disorders is a clinical psychologist.
Family therapy	Family therapy is a branch of psychotherapy that treats family problems. Family therapists consider the family as a system of interacting members; as such, the problems in the family are seen to arise as an emergent property of the interactions in the system, rather than ascribed exclusively to the "faults" or psychological problems of individual members.
Existential therapy	Existential therapy is partly based on the belief that human beings are alone in the world. This aloneness leads to feelings of meaninglessness which can be overcome only by creating one's own values and meanings. We have the power to create because we have the freedom to choose.
Charcot	Charcot took an interest in the malady then called hysteria. It seemed to be a mental disorder with physical manifestations, of immediate interest to a neurologist. He believed that hysteria was the result of a weak neurological system which was hereditary.
Hysteria	Hysteria is a diagnostic label applied to a state of mind, one of unmanageable fear or emotional excesses. The fear is often centered on a body part, most often on an imagined problem with that body part.
Hypnosis	Hypnosis is a psychological state whose existence and effects are strongly debated. Some believe that it is a state under which the subject's mind becomes so suggestible that the hypnotist, the one who induces the state, can establish communication with the subconscious mind of the subject and command behavior that the subject would not choose to perform in a conscious state.
Breuer	Breuer is perhaps best known for his work with Anna O. – a woman suffering with symptoms of paralysis, anaesthesias, and disturbances of vision and speech. The discussions of Anna O. between Freud and Breuer were documented in their Studies in Hysteria and became a formative basis of Freudian theory and psychoanalytic practice.
Attachment	Attachment is the tendency to seek closeness to another person and feel secure when that person is present.
Psychoanalyst	A psychoanalyst is a specially trained therapist who attempts to treat the individual by uncovering and revealing to the individual otherwise subconscious factors that are contributing to some undesirable behavor.
Theories	Theories are logically self-consistent models or frameworks describing the behavior of a

	certain natural or social phenomenon. They are broad explanations and predictions concerning phenomena of interest.
Otto Rank	Otto Rank extended psychoanalytic theory to the study of legend, myth, art, and other works of creativity. He favored a more egalitarian relationship with patients and is sometimes considered the forerunner of client-centered therapy.
Adler	Adler argued that human personality could be explained teleologically, separate strands dominated by the guiding purpose of the individual's unconscious self ideal to convert feelings of inferiority to superiority (or rather completeness). The desires of the self ideal were countered by social and ethical demands.
Jung	Jung was in some aspects a response to Sigmund Freud's psychoanalysis. He proposed and developed the concepts of the extroverted and introverted personality, archetypes, and the collective unconscious. His work has been influential in psychiatry and in the study of religion, literature, and related fields.
Determinism	Determinism is the philosophical proposition that every event, including human cognition and action, is causally determined by an unbroken chain of prior occurrences.
Motivation	In psychology, motivation is the driving force (desire) behind all actions of an organism.
Death instinct	The death instinct was defined by Sigmund Freud, in Beyond the Pleasure Principle(1920). It speculated on the existence of a fundamental death wish or death instinct, referring to an individual's own need to die.
Instinct	Instinct is the word used to describe inherent dispositions towards particular actions. They are generally an inherited pattern of responses or reactions to certain kinds of situations.
Thanatos	In psychoanalytical theory, Thanatos is the death instinct, which opposes Eros. The "death instinct" identified by Sigmund Freud, which signals a desire to give up the struggle of life and return to quiescence and the grave.
Eros	In Freudian psychology, Eros is the life instinct innate in all humans. It is the desire to create life and favours productivity and construction. Eros battles against the destructive death instinct of Thanatos.
Attention	Attention is the cognitive process of selectively concentrating on one thing while ignoring other things. Psychologists have labeled three types of attention: sustained attention, selective attention, and divided attention.
Superego	Frued's third psychic structure, which functions as a moral guardian and sets forth high standards for behavior is the superego.
Ego	In Freud's view the Ego serves to balance our primitive needs and our moral beliefs and taboos. Relying on experience, a healthy Ego provides the ability to adapt to reality and interact with the outside world.
Pleasure principle	The pleasure principle is the tendency to seek pleasure and avoid pain. In Freud's theory, this principle rules the Id, but is at least partly repressed by the reality principle.
Primary process	The primary process in psychoanalytic theory, is one of the id's means of reducing tension by imagining what it desires.
Mental Representation	Stage six of the sensorimotor substages, Mental representation, 18 months to 2 years, marks the beginnings of insight, or true creativity. This marks the passage into unique thought in Piaget's later three areas of development.
Psychotherapy	Psychotherapy is a set of techniques based on psychological principles intended to improve mental health, emotional or behavioral issues.

Psychodynamic	Most psychodynamic approaches are centered around the idea of a maladapted function developed early in life (usually childhood) which are at least in part unconscious. This maladapted function (a.k.a. defense mechanism) does not do well in place of a normal/healthy one.
Perception	Perception is the process of acquiring, interpreting, selecting, and organizing sensory information.
Learning	Learning is a relatively permanent change in behavior that results from experience. Thus, to attribute a behavioral change to learning, the change must be relatively permanent and must result from experience.
Reality principle	The reality principle tells us to subordinate pleasure to what needs to be done. Subordinating the pleasure principle to the reality principle is done through a psychological process Freud calls sublimation, where you take desires that can't be fulfilled, or shouldn't be fulfilled, and turn their energy into something useful and productive.
Secondary process	Secondary process is the mental activity and thinking characteristic of the ego, influenced by the demands of the environment. Characterized by organization, systematization, intellectualization, and similar processes leading to logical thought and action in adult life.
Oedipus complex	The Oedipus complex is a concept developed by Sigmund Freud to explain the maturation of the infant boy through identification with the father and desire for the mother.
Society	The social sciences use the term society to mean a group of people that form a semi-closed (or semi-open) social system, in which most interactions are with other individuals belonging to the group.
Ego ideal	The component of the superego that involves ideal standards approved by parents is called ego ideal. The ego ideal rewards the child by conveying a sense of pride and personal value when the child acts according to ideal standards.
Shaping	The concept of reinforcing successive, increasingly accurate approximations to a target behavior is called shaping. The target behavior is broken down into a hierarchy of elemental steps, each step more sophisticated then the last. By successively reinforcing each of the the elemental steps, a form of differential reinforcement, until that step is learned while extinguishing the step below, the target behavior is gradually achieved.
Erogenous zone	An erogenous zone is an area of the human body that has heightened sensitivity and stimulation normally results in sexual response.
Oral stage	The oral stage in psychology is the term used by Sigmund Freud to describe the development during the first eighteen months of life, in which an infant's pleasure centers are in the mouth. This is the first of Freud's psychosexual stages.
Stages	Stages represent relatively discrete periods of time in which functioning is qualitatively different from functioning at other periods.
Psychosexual stages	In Freudian theory each child passes through five psychosexual stages. During each stage, the id focuses on a distinct erogenous zone on the body. Suffering from trauma during any of the first three stages may result in fixation in that stage. Freud related the resolutions of the stages with adult personalities and personality disorders.
Anal stage	The anal stage in psychology is the term used by Sigmund Freud to describe the development during the second year of life, in which a child's pleasure and conflict centers are in the anal area.
Latency stage	Sigmund Freud suggested that the latency stage, age 6-10, this was a time of sexual latency, when the healthy child ceased all sexual interest and was vulnerable to trauma if he or she experienced sexuality.

Latency	In child development, latency refers to a phase of psychosexual development characterized by repression of sexual impulses. In learning theory, latency is the delay between stimulus (S) and response (R), which according to Hull depends on the strength of the association.
Genital stage	The genital stage in psychology is the term used by Sigmund Freud to describe the final stage of human psychosexual development. It is characterized by the expression of libido through intercourse with an adult of the other gender.
Adolescence	The period of life bounded by puberty and the assumption of adult responsibilities is adolescence.
Maladjustment	Maladjustment is the condition of being unable to adapt properly to your environment with resulting emotional instability.
Reaction formation	In Freud's psychoanalytic theory, reaction formation is a defense mechanism in which anxiety-producing or unacceptable emotions are replaced by their direct opposites.
Sublimation	Sublimation is a coping mechanism. It refers to rechanneling sexual or aggressive energy into pursuits that society considers acceptable or admirable.
Affective	Affective is the way people react emotionally, their ability to feel another living thing's pain or joy.
Anxiety	Anxiety is a complex combination of the feeling of fear, apprehension and worry often accompanied by physical sensations such as palpitations, chest pain and/or shortness of breath.
Lungs	The lungs are the essential organs of respiration. Its principal function is to transport oxygen from the atmosphere into the bloodstream, and excrete carbon dioxide from the bloodstream into the atmosphere.
Neurotic anxiety	Neurotic anxiety refers to, in psychoanalytic theory, a fear of the consequences of expressing previously punished and repressed id impulses; more generally, unrealistic fear.
Moral anxiety	In psychoanalytic theory, the ego's fear of punishment for failure to adhere to the superego's standards of proper conduct is referred to as moral anxiety.
Defense mechanism	A Defense mechanism is a set of unconscious ways to protect one's personality from unpleasant thoughts and realities which may otherwise cause anxiety. The notion is an integral part of the psychoanalytic theory.
Consciousness	The awareness of the sensations, thoughts, and feelings being experienced at a given moment is called consciousness.
Fixation	Fixation in abnormal psychology is the state where an individual becomes obsessed with an attachment to another human, animal or inanimate object. Fixation in vision refers to maintaining the gaze in a constant direction. .
Psychosexual development	In psychodynamic theory, the process by which libidinal energy is expressed through different erogenous zones during different stages of development is called psychosexual development.
Regression	Return to a form of behavior characteristic of an earlier stage of development is called regression.
Projection	Attributing one's own undesirable thoughts, impulses, traits, or behaviors to others is referred to as projection.
Free association	In psychoanalysis, the uncensored uttering of all thoughts that come to mind is called free association.
Insight	Insight refers to a sudden awareness of the relationships among various elements that had previously appeared to be independent of one another.

Flooding	Flooding is a behavioral fear-reduction technique based on principles of classical conditioning. Fear-evoking stimuli are presented continuously in the absence of harm so that fear responses are extinguished. However, subjects tend to avoid the stimulus, making extinction difficult.
Emotion	An emotion is a mental states that arise spontaneously, rather than through conscious effort. They are often accompanied by physiological changes.
Affect	A subjective feeling or emotional tone often accompanied by bodily expressions noticeable to others is called affect.
Neurosis	Neurosis, any mental disorder that, although may cause distress, does not interfere with rational thought or the persons' ability to function.
Psychodynamic psychotherapy	The "goal" of psychodynamic therapy is the experience of "truth." This "truth" must be encountered through the breakdown of psychological defenses. Psychodynamic psychotherapy involves a great idea of introspection and reflection from the client.
Phobia	A persistent, irrational fear of an object, situation, or activity that the person feels compelled to avoid is referred to as a phobia.
Trait	An enduring personality characteristic that tends to lead to certain behaviors is called a trait. The term trait also means a genetically inherited feature of an organism.
Unconscious thought	Unconscious thought is Freud's concept of a reservoir of unacceptable wishes, feelings, and thoughts that are beyond conscious awareness.
Early childhood	Early childhood refers to the developmental period extending from the end of infancy to about 5 or 6 years of age; sometimes called the preschool years.
Wish fulfillment	A primitive method used by the id to attempt to gratify basic instincts is referred to as wish fulfillment.
Manifest content	In psychodynamic theory, the reported content of dreams is referred to as manifest content.
Latent content	In psychodynamic theory, the symbolized or underlying content of dreams is called latent content.
Symbolization	In Bandura's social cognitive theory, the ability to think about one's social behavior in terms of words and images is referred to as symbolization. Symbolization allows us to translate a transient experience into a guide for future action.
Displacement	An unconscious defense mechanism in which the individual directs aggressive or sexual feelings away from the primary object to someone or something safe is referred to as displacement. Displacement in linguistics is simply the ability to talk about things not present.
Attitude	An enduring mental representation of a person, place, or thing that evokes an emotional response and related behavior is called attitude.
Transference	Transference is a phenomenon in psychology characterized by unconscious redirection of feelings from one person to another.
Motives	Needs or desires that energize and direct behavior toward a goal are motives.
Ego analyst	A psychodynamically oriented therapist who focuses on the conscious, coping behavior of the ego instead of the hypothesized, unconscious functioning of the id is referred to as an ego analyst.
Birth trauma	Birth trauma refers to injury or disturbing experiences sustained at the time of birth.
Trauma	Trauma refers to a severe physical injury or wound to the body caused by an external force,

	or a psychological shock having a lasting effect on mental life.
Sullivan	Sullivan developed the Self System, a configuration of the personality traits developed in childhood and reinforced by positive affirmation and the security operations developed in childhood to avoid anxiety and threats to self-esteem.
Maturation	The orderly unfolding of traits, as regulated by the genetic code is called maturation.
Kohut	Kohut was a pioneer in the fields of psychology and psychiatry. He established the school of Self Psychology as a branch of psychoanalysis. Where Freud empahasized guilt in the etiology of emotional disorders, Kohut saw shame as more central.
Brief therapy	A primary approach of brief therapy is to open up the present to admit a wider context and more appropriate understandings (not necessarily at a conscious level), rather than formal analysis of historical causes.
Psychodynamic therapy	Psychodynamic therapy uses a range of different techniques, applied to the client considering his or her needs. Most approaches are centered around the idea of a maladapted function developed early in life which are at least in part unconscious.
Psychiatrist	A psychiatrist is a physician who specializes in the diagnosis and treatment of psychological disorders.
American Psychological Association	The American Psychological Association is a professional organization representing psychology in the US. The mission statement is to "advance psychology as a science and profession and as a means of promoting health, education , and human welfare".
Individual differences	Individual differences psychology studies the ways in which individual people differ in their behavior. This is distinguished from other aspects of psychology in that although psychology is ostensibly a study of individuals, modern psychologists invariably study groups.
Therapeutic alliance	A therapeutic alliance refers to a caring relationship that unites a therapist and a client in working to solve the client's problems.
Empirical	Empirical means the use of working hypotheses which are capable of being disproved using observation or experiment.
Pragmatism	Pragmatism is characterized by the insistence on consequences, utility and practicality as vital components of truth. Pragmatism objects to the view that human concepts and intellect represent reality, and therefore stands in opposition to both formalist and rationalist schools of philosophy.
Parsimony	In science, parsimony is preference for the least complicated explanation for an observation. This is generally regarded as good when judging hypotheses. Occam's Razor also states the "principle of parsimony".
Presenting problem	The presenting problem is the original complaint reported by the client to the therapist. The actual treated problem may sometimes be a modification derived from the presenting problem or entirely different..
Pathology	Pathology is the study of the processes underlying disease and other forms of illness, harmful abnormality, or dysfunction.
Substance abuse	Substance abuse refers to the overindulgence in and dependence on a stimulant, depressant, or other chemical substance, leading to effects that are detrimental to the individual's physical or mental health, or the welfare of others.
Bulimia	Bulimia refers to a disorder in which a person binges on incredibly large quantities of food, then purges by vomiting or by using laxatives. Bulimia is often less about food, and more to do with deep psychological issues and profound feelings of lack of control.

Interpersonal psychotherapy | A brief treatment approach that emphasizes resolution of interpersonal problems and stressors such as role disputes in marital conflict, or forming relationships in marriage or a new job is referred to as interpersonal psychotherapy.

Depressive disorders | Depressive disorders are mood disorders in which the individual suffers depression without ever experiencing mania.

Personality trait | According to the Diagnostic and Statistical Manual of the American Psychiatric Association, a personality trait is a "prominent aspect of personality that is exhibited in a wide range of important social and personal contexts. ...".

Depression | In everyday language depression refers to any downturn in mood, which may be relatively transitory and perhaps due to something trivial. This is differentiated from Clinical depression which is marked by symptoms that last two weeks or more and are so severe that they interfere with daily living.

Autonomy | Autonomy is the condition of something that does not depend on anything else.

Adaptive behavior | An adaptive behavior increases the probability of the individual or organism to survive or exist within its environment.

Clinical psychology | Clinical psychology is involved in the diagnosis, assessment, and treatment of patients with mental or behavioral disorders, and conducts research in these various areas.

Population | Population refers to all members of a well-defined group of organisms, events, or things.

Psyche | Psyche is the soul, spirit, or mind as distinguished from the body. In psychoanalytic theory, it is the totality of the id, ego, and superego, including both conscious and unconscious components.

Clinician | A health professional authorized to provide services to people suffering from one or more pathologies is a clinician.

Empirical evidence | Facts or information based on direct observation or experience are referred to as empirical evidence.

Positive relationship | Statistically, a positive relationship refers to a mathematical relationship in which increases in one measure are matched by increases in the other.

Object relation | Object relation theory is the idea that the ego-self exists only in relation to other objects, which may be external or internal.

Hypothesis | A specific statement about behavior or mental processes that is testable through research is a hypothesis.

Variable | A variable refers to a measurable factor, characteristic, or attribute of an individual or a system.

Behavioral therapy | The treatment of a mental disorder through the application of basic principles of conditioning and learning is called behavioral therapy.

Agoraphobia | An irrational fear of open, crowded places is called agoraphobia. Many people suffering from agoraphobia, however, are not afraid of the open spaces themselves, but of situations often associated with these spaces, such as social gatherings.

Brief psychodynamic therapy | A modern therapy based on psychoanalytic theory but designed to produce insights more quickly is brief psychodynamic therapy.

Catharsis | Catharsis has been adopted by modern psychotherapy as the act of giving expression to deep emotions often associated with events in the individuals past which have never before been adequately expressed.

Innate	Innate behavior is not learned or influenced by the environment, rather, it is present or predisposed at birth.
Phallic stage	The phallic stage is the 3rd of Freud's psychosexual stages, when awareness of and manipulation of the genitals is supposed to be a primary source of pleasure. In this stage the child deals with the Oedipus complex, if male, or the Electra Complex, if female.
Repression	A defense mechanism, repression involves moving thoughts unacceptable to the ego into the unconscious, where they cannot be easily accessed.

Insight	Insight refers to a sudden awareness of the relationships among various elements that had previously appeared to be independent of one another.
Psychoanalytic	Freud's theory that unconscious forces act as determinants of personality is called psychoanalytic theory. The theory is a developmental theory characterized by critical stages of development.
Psychotherapy	Psychotherapy is a set of techniques based on psychological principles intended to improve mental health, emotional or behavioral issues.
Psychoanalysis	Psychoanalysis refers to the school of psychology that emphasizes the importance of unconscious motives and conflicts as determinants of human behavior. It was Freud's method of exploring human personality.
Carl Rogers	Carl Rogers was instrumental in the development of non-directive psychotherapy, also known as "client-centered" psychotherapy. Rogers' basic tenets were unconditional positive regard, genuineness, and empathic understanding, with each demonstrated by the counselor.
Theories	Theories are logically self-consistent models or frameworks describing the behavior of a certain natural or social phenomenon. They are broad explanations and predictions concerning phenomena of interest.
Personality	Personality refers to the pattern of enduring characteristics that differentiates a person, the patterns of behaviors that make each individual unique.
Attention	Attention is the cognitive process of selectively concentrating on one thing while ignoring other things. Psychologists have labeled three types of attention: sustained attention, selective attention, and divided attention.
Allport	Allport was a trait theorist. Those traits he believed to predominate a person's personality were called central traits. Traits such that one could be indentifed by the trait, were referred to as cardinal traits. Central traits and cardinal traits are influenced by environmental factors.
Lewin	Lewin ranks as one of the pioneers of social psychology, as one of the founders of group dynamics and as one of the most eminent representatives of Gestalt psychology.
Clinical psychologist	A psychologist, usually with a Ph.D, whose training is in the diagnosis, treatment, or research of psychological and behavioral disorders is a clinical psychologist.
Otto Rank	Otto Rank extended psychoanalytic theory to the study of legend, myth, art, and other works of creativity. He favored a more egalitarian relationship with patients and is sometimes considered the forerunner of client-centered therapy.
Inference	Inference is the act or process of drawing a conclusion based solely on what one already knows.
Population	Population refers to all members of a well-defined group of organisms, events, or things.
Humanistic	Humanistic refers to any system of thought focused on subjective experience and human problems and potentials.
Clinician	A health professional authorized to provide services to people suffering from one or more pathologies is a clinician.
Learning	Learning is a relatively permanent change in behavior that results from experience. Thus, to attribute a behavioral change to learning, the change must be relatively permanent and must result from experience.
Symbolization	In Bandura's social cognitive theory, the ability to think about one's social behavior in terms of words and images is referred to as symbolization. Symbolization allows us to

	translate a transient experience into a guide for future action.
Unconditional positive regard	Unqualified caring and nonjudgmental acceptance of another is called unconditional positive regard.
Empathic understanding	Empathic understanding refers to ability to perceive a client's feelings from the client's frame of reference.
Empathy	Empathy is the recognition and understanding of the states of mind, including beliefs, desires and particularly emotions of others without injecting your own.
Attitude	An enduring mental representation of a person, place, or thing that evokes an emotional response and related behavior is called attitude.
Consciousness	The awareness of the sensations, thoughts, and feelings being experienced at a given moment is called consciousness.
Prognosis	A forecast about the probable course of an illess is referred to as prognosis.
Accurate empathic understanding	In client-centered therapy, an essential quality of the therapist is an accurate empathic understanding or the ability to see the world through the client's phenomenology as well as from perspectives of which the client may be only dimly aware .
Psychoanalyst	A psychoanalyst is a specially trained therapist who attempts to treat the individual by uncovering and revealing to the individual otherwise subconscious factors that are contributing to some undesirable behavor.
Reflection	Reflection is the process of rephrasing or repeating thoughts and feelings expressed, making the person more aware of what they are saying or thinking.
Stages	Stages represent relatively discrete periods of time in which functioning is qualitatively different from functioning at other periods.
Emotion	An emotion is a mental states that arise spontaneously, rather than through conscious effort. They are often accompanied by physiological changes.
Denial	Denial is a psychological defense mechanism in which a person faced with a fact that is uncomfortable or painful to accept rejects it instead, insisting that it is not true despite what may be overwhelming evidence.
Validity	The extent to which a test measures what it is intended to measure is called validity.
Autonomy	Autonomy is the condition of something that does not depend on anything else.
Paraprofessional	A paraprofessional is an individual lacking a doctoral degree but trained to perform certain functions usually reserved for clinicians.
Instinct	Instinct is the word used to describe inherent dispositions towards particular actions. They are generally an inherited pattern of responses or reactions to certain kinds of situations.
Transference	Transference is a phenomenon in psychology characterized by unconscious redirection of feelings from one person to another.
Effect size	An effect size is the strength or magnitude of the difference between two sets of data or, in outcome studies, between two time points for the same population. (The degree to which the null hypothesis is false).
Control group	A group that does not receive the treatment effect in an experiment is referred to as the control group or sometimes as the comparison group.
Stimulus	A change in an environmental condition that elicits a response is a stimulus.
Wisdom	Wisdom is the ability to make correct judgments and decisions. It is an intangible quality

gained through experience. Whether or not something is wise is determined in a pragmatic sense by its popularity, how long it has been around, and its ability to predict against future events.

Authoritarian — The term authoritarian is used to describe a style that enforces strong and sometimes oppressive measures against those in its sphere of influence, generally without attempts at gaining their consent.

Psychosis — Psychosis is a generic term for mental states in which the components of rational thought and perception are severely impaired. Persons experiencing a psychosis may experience hallucinations, hold paranoid or delusional beliefs, demonstrate personality changes and exhibit disorganized thinking. This is usually accompanied by features such as a lack of insight into the unusual or bizarre nature of their behavior, difficulties with social interaction and impairments in carrying out the activities of daily living.

Humanism — Humanism refers to the philosophy and school of psychology that asserts that people are conscious, self-aware, and capable of free choice, self-fulfillment, and ethical behavior.

Existentialism — The view that people are completely free and responsible for their own behavior is existentialism.

Phenomenology — Phenomenology is the study of subjective mental experiences; a theme of humanistic theories of personality. It studies meaningful, intact mental events without dividing them for further analysis.

Humanistic psychology — Humanistic psychology refers to the school of psychology that focuses on the uniqueness of human beings and their capacity for choice, growth, and psychological health.

Behaviorism — The school of psychology that defines psychology as the study of observable behavior and studies relationships between stimuli and responses is called behaviorism. Behaviorism relied heavily on animal research and stated the same principles governed the behavior of both nonhumans and humans.

Determinism — Determinism is the philosophical proposition that every event, including human cognition and action, is causally determined by an unbroken chain of prior occurrences.

Construct — A generalized concept, such as anxiety or gravity, is a construct.

Intuition — Quick, impulsive thought that does not make use of formal logic or clear reasoning is referred to as intuition.

Norms — In testing, standards of test performance that permit the comparison of one person's score on the test to the scores of others who have taken the same test are referred to as norms.

Maslow — Maslow is mostly noted today for his proposal of a hierarchy of human needs which he often presented as a pyramid. Maslow was an instrumental player in the formation of the humanistic movement, also known as the third force in psychology.

Existential psychology — Existential psychology is partly based on the belief that human beings are alone in the world. This aloneness leads to feelings of meaninglessness which can be overcome only by creating one's own values and meanings

Existential therapy — Existential therapy is partly based on the belief that human beings are alone in the world. This aloneness leads to feelings of meaninglessness which can be overcome only by creating one's own values and meanings. We have the power to create because we have the freedom to choose.

Society — The social sciences use the term society to mean a group of people that form a semi-closed (or semi-open) social system, in which most interactions are with other individuals belonging to the group.

Kierkegaard | Kierkegaard has achieved general recognition as the first existentialist philosopher, though some new research shows this may be a more difficult connection than previously thought.

Heidegger | Heidegger is regarded as a major influence on existentialism. He focused on the phenomenon of intentionality. Human behavior is intentional insofar as it is directed at some object or end (all building is building of something, all talking is talking about something, etc).

Binswanger | Binswanger is considered the founder of existential psychology. In the early 1920s he turned increasingly towards an existential rather than Freudian perspective, so that by the early 1930s he had become the first existential therapist.

Human nature | Human nature is the fundamental nature and substance of humans, as well as the range of human behavior that is believed to be invariant over long periods of time and across very different cultural contexts.

Guilt | Guilt describes many concepts related to a negative emotion or condition caused by actions which are believed to be, morally wrong. According to Freud, the avoidance of guilt is the basis for moral behavior.

Anxiety | Anxiety is a complex combination of the feeling of fear, apprehension and worry often accompanied by physical sensations such as palpitations, chest pain and/or shortness of breath.

Logotherapy | Developed by Viktor Frankl, Logotherapy is considered the "third Viennese school of psychotherapy" after Freud's psychoanalysis and Adler's individual psychology. It is a type of Existential Analysis that focuses on a "will to meaning" as opposed to Adler's Nietzschian doctrine of "will to power" or Freud's of "will to pleasure".

Paradoxical | Paradoxical intention refers to instructing clients to do the opposite of the desired behavior. Telling an impotent man not to have sex or an insomniac not to sleep reduces anxiety to perform.

Gestalt therapy | Gestalt therapy is a form of psychotherapy, based on the experiential ideal of "here and now," and relationships with others and the world. By focusing the individual on their self-awareness as part of present reality, new insights can be made into their behavior, and they can engage in self-healing.

Wertheimer | His discovery of the phi phenomenon concerning the illusion of motion gave rise to the influential school of Gestalt psychology. In the latter part of his life, Wertheimer directed much of his attention to the problem of learning.

Koffka | Koffka was cofounder of the Gestalt school of psychology. They stressed the approach that psychological phenomena cannot be interpreted as combinations of elements: parts derive their meaning from the whole, and people perceive complex entities rather than their elements.

Kohler | Kohler applied Gestalt principles to study chimpanzees and recorded their ability to devise and use tools and solve problems. In 1917, he published and gained fame with The Mentality of Apes, in which he argued that his subjects, like humans, were capable of insight learning. His work led to a radical revision of learning theory.

Cognition | The intellectual processes through which information is obtained, transformed, stored, retrieved, and otherwise used is cognition.

Superego | Frued's third psychic structure, which functions as a moral guardian and sets forth high standards for behavior is the superego.

Hedonism | The motivation of humans and other animals to seek pleasure and avoid pain is referred to as hedonism.

Watson | Watson, the father of behaviorism, developed the term "Behaviorism" as a name for his

	proposal to revolutionize the study of human psychology in order to put it on a firm experimental footing.
Habit	A habit is a response that has become completely separated from its eliciting stimulus. Early learning theorists used the term to describe S-R associations, however not all S-R associations become a habit, rather many are extinguished after reinforcement is withdrawn.
Free will	The idea that human beings are capable of freely making choices or decisions is free will.
Encounter group	A type of group that fosters self-awareness by focusing on how group members relate to one another in a setting that encourages open expression of feelings is called an encounter group.
Humanistic movement	The humanistic movement places emphasis on a person's capacity for personal growth, freedom to choose a destiny, and positive qualities.
Subjective experience	Subjective experience refers to reality as it is perceived and interpreted, not as it exists objectively.
Bias	A bias is a prejudice in a general or specific sense, usually in the sense for having a preference to one particular point of view or ideological perspective.
Cohesiveness	Cohesiveness with respect to conformity is the degree of attraction felt by an individual toward an influencing group.
Peak experiences	Temporary moments of self-actualization are peak experiences.
Neologism	A neologism is word, term, or phrase which has been recently created ("coined") —often to apply to new concepts, or to reshape older terms in newer language form. They are especially useful in identifying inventions, new phenomena, or old ideas which have taken on a new cultural context.
Empirical	Empirical means the use of working hypotheses which are capable of being disproved using observation or experiment.
Perception	Perception is the process of acquiring, interpreting, selecting, and organizing sensory information.
Free choice	Free choice refers to the ability to freely make choices that are not controlled by genetics, learning, or unconscious forces.

Behavior therapy | Behavior therapy refers to the systematic application of the principles of learning to direct modification of a client's problem behaviors.

Rubric | In education, a rubric is a set of criteria and standards linked to learning objectives that is used to assess a student's performance on a paper, project, essay, etc.

Conditioning | Conditioning describes the process by which behaviors can be learned or modified through interaction with the environment.

Learning | Learning is a relatively permanent change in behavior that results from experience. Thus, to attribute a behavioral change to learning, the change must be relatively permanent and must result from experience.

Skinner | Skinner conducted research on shaping behavior through positive and negative reinforcement, and demonstrated operant conditioning, a technique which he developed in contrast with classical conditioning.

Wolpe | Wolpe is best known for applying classical conditioning principles to the treatment of phobias, called systematic desensitization. Any "neutral" stimulus, simple or complex that happens to make an impact on an individual at about the time that a fear reaction is evoked acquires the ability to evoke fear subsequently. An acquired CS-CR relationship should be extinguishable.

Classical conditioning | Classical conditioning is a simple form of learning in which an organism comes to associate or anticipate events. A neutral stimulus comes to evoke the response usually evoked by a natural or unconditioned stimulus by being paired repeatedly with the unconditioned stimulus.

Operant Conditioning | A simple form of learning in which an organism learns to engage in behavior because it is reinforced is referred to as operant conditioning. The consequences of a behavior produce changes in the probability of the behavior's occurence.

Variable | A variable refers to a measurable factor, characteristic, or attribute of an individual or a system.

Pavlov | Pavlov first described the phenomenon now known as classical conditioning in experiments with dogs.

Laboratory study | Any research study in which the subjects are brought to a specially designated area that has been set up to facilitate the researcher's ability to control the environment or collect data is referred to as a laboratory study.

Watson | Watson, the father of behaviorism, developed the term "Behaviorism" as a name for his proposal to revolutionize the study of human psychology in order to put it on a firm experimental footing.

Pavlovian conditioning | Pavlovian conditioning, synonymous with classical conditioning is a type of learning found in animals, caused by the association (or pairing) of two stimuli or what Ivan Pavlov described as the learning of conditional behavior, therefore called conditioning.

Neutral stimulus | A stimulus prior to conditioning that does not naturally result in the response of interest is called a neutral stimulus.

Stimulus | A change in an environmental condition that elicits a response is a stimulus.

Mary Cover Jones | Mary Cover Jones stands out as a pioneer of behavior therapy. Her study of unconditioning a fear of rabbits in a three-year-old named Peter is her most often cited work.

Antecedents | In behavior modification, events that typically precede the target response are called antecedents.

Reciprocal | The concept of reciprocal inhibition states that presence of one emotional state can inhibit

inhibition	the occurrence of another, such as joy preventing fear or anxiety inhibiting pleasure.
Psychotherapy	Psychotherapy is a set of techniques based on psychological principles intended to improve mental health, emotional or behavioral issues.
Hans Eysenck	Hans Eysenck using Factor Analysis concluded that all human traits can be broken down into two distinct categories: 1. Extroversion-Introversion, 2. Neuroticism. He called these categories Supertraits.
Acquisition	Acquisition is the process of adapting to the environment, learning or becoming conditioned. In classical conditoning terms, it is the initial learning of the stimulus response link, which involves a neutral stimulus being associated with a unconditioned stimulus and becoming a conditioned stimulus.
Anxiety	Anxiety is a complex combination of the feeling of fear, apprehension and worry often accompanied by physical sensations such as palpitations, chest pain and/or shortness of breath.
Desensitization	Desensitization refers to the type of sensory or behavioral adaptation in which we become less sensitive to constant stimuli.
Systematic desensitization	Systematic desensitization refers to Wolpe's behavioral fear-reduction technique in which a hierarchy of fear-evoking stimuli are presented while the person remains relaxed. The fear-evoking stimuli thereby become associated with muscle relaxation.
Reflex	A simple, involuntary response to a stimulus is referred to as reflex. Reflex actions originate at the spinal cord rather than the brain.
Conditioned reflex	The conditioned reflex was Pavlov's term for the conditioned response which is a an acquired response that is under the control of (conditional on the occurrence of) a stimulus
Demonology	Demonology refers to the doctrine that a person's abnormal behavior is caused by an autonomous evil spirit.
Motivation	In psychology, motivation is the driving force (desire) behind all actions of an organism.
Rotter	Rotter focused on the application of social learning theory (SLT) to clinical psychology. She introduced the ideas of learning from generalized expectancies of reinforcement and internal/ external locus of control (self-initiated change versus change influenced by others). According to Rotter, health outcomes could be improved by the development of a sense of personal control over one's life.
Empirical	Empirical means the use of working hypotheses which are capable of being disproved using observation or experiment.
Behavioral therapy	The treatment of a mental disorder through the application of basic principles of conditioning and learning is called behavioral therapy.
Clinical psychologist	A psychologist, usually with a Ph.D, whose training is in the diagnosis, treatment, or research of psychological and behavioral disorders is a clinical psychologist.
Cognitive approach	A cognitive approach focuses on the mental processes involved in knowing: how we direct our attention, perceive, remember, think, and solve problems.
Behavioral assessment	Direct measures of an individual's behavior used to describe characteristics indicative of personality are called behavioral assessment.
Social anxiety	A feeling of apprehension in the presence of others is social anxiety.
Phobia	A persistent, irrational fear of an object, situation, or activity that the person feels compelled to avoid is referred to as a phobia.

Questionnaire	A self-report method of data collection or clinical assessment method in which the individual being studied checks off items on a printed list, answers multiple-choice questions, or writes out answers to essay questions aimed at producing a selfdescription is called questionnaire.
Clinician	A health professional authorized to provide services to people suffering from one or more pathologies is a clinician.
Sensation	Sensation is the first stage in the chain of biochemical and neurologic events that begins with the impinging of a stimulus upon the receptor cells of a sensory organ, which then leads to perception, the mental state that is reflected in statements like "I see a uniformly blue wall."
Relaxation training	Relaxation training is an intervention technique used for tics. The person is taught to relax the muscles involved in the tics.
Hypnosis	Hypnosis is a psychological state whose existence and effects are strongly debated. Some believe that it is a state under which the subject's mind becomes so suggestible that the hypnotist, the one who induces the state, can establish communication with the subconscious mind of the subject and command behavior that the subject would not choose to perform in a conscious state.
Construct	A generalized concept, such as anxiety or gravity, is a construct.
Neurotic anxiety	Neurotic anxiety refers to, in psychoanalytic theory, a fear of the consequences of expressing previously punished and repressed id impulses; more generally, unrealistic fear.
Extinction	In operant extinction, if no reinforcement is delivered after the response, gradually the behavior will no longer occur in the presence of the stimulus. The process is more rapid following continuous reinforcement rather than after partial reinforcement. In Classical Conditioning, repeated presentations of the CS without being followed by the US results in the extinction of the CS.
Countercondi-ioning	The process of eliminating a classically conditioned response by pairing the CS with an unconditioned stimulus for a response that is stronger than the conditioned response and that cannot occur at the same time as the CR is called counterconditioning.
Arousal	Arousal is a physiological and psychological state involving the activation of the reticular activating system in the brain stem, the autonomic nervous system and the endocrine system, leading to increased heart rate and blood pressure and a condition of alertness and readiness to respond.
Reinforcement	In operant conditioning, reinforcement is any change in an environment that (a) occurs after the behavior, (b) seems to make that behavior re-occur more often in the future and (c) that reoccurence of behavior must be the result of the change.
Positive reinforcement	In positive reinforcement, a stimulus is added and the rate of responding increases.
Exposure therapy	An exposure therapy is any method of treating fears, including flooding and systematic desensitization, that involves exposing the client to the feared object or situation so that the process of extinction or habituation of the fear response can occur.
Anxiety disorder	Anxiety disorder is a blanket term covering several different forms of abnormal anxiety, fear, phobia and nervous condition, that come on suddenly and prevent pursuing normal daily routines.
Specific phobia	A specific phobia is a generic term for anxiety disorders that amount to unreasonable or irrational fear or anxiety related with exposure to specific objects or situations. As a result, the affected persons tend to actively avoid these objects or situations.

Panic disorder	A panic attack is a period of intense fear or discomfort, typically with an abrupt onset and usually lasting no more than thirty minutes. The disorder is strikingly different from other types of anxiety, in that panic attacks are very sudden, appear to be unprovoked, and are often disabling. People who have repeated attacks, or feel severe anxiety about having another attack are said to have panic disorder.
Generalized anxiety disorder	Generalized anxiety disorder is an anxiety disorder that is characterized by uncontrollable worry about everyday things. The frequency, intensity, and duration of the worry are disproportionate to the actual source of worry, and such worry often interferes with daily functioning.
Exposure treatment	An exposure treatment is any method of treating fears, including flooding and systematic desensitization, that involves exposing the client to the feared object or situation so that the process of extinction or habituation of the fear response can occur.
Panic attack	An attack of overwhelming anxiety, fear, or terror is called panic attack.
Relearning	Relearning refers to a measure of retention used in experiments on memory. Material is usually relearned more quickly than it is learned initially.
Implosion	A behavioral treatment that attempts to extinguish a fear by having the client imagine the anxiety siituation at its maximum intensity is called implosion.
Flooding	Flooding is a behavioral fear-reduction technique based on principles of classical conditioning. Fear-evoking stimuli are presented continuously in the absence of harm so that fear responses are extinguished. However, subjects tend to avoid the stimulus, making extinction difficult.
Stress disorder	A significant emotional disturbance caused by stresses outside the range of normal human experience is referred to as stress disorder.
Social phobia	An irrational, excessive fear of public scrutiny is referred to as social phobia.
Agoraphobia	An irrational fear of open, crowded places is called agoraphobia. Many people suffering from agoraphobia, however, are not afraid of the open spaces themselves, but of situations often associated with these spaces, such as social gatherings.
In vivo	In vivo is used to indicate the presence of a whole/living organism, in distinction to a partial or dead organism, or a computer model. In vivo research is more suited to observe an overall effect than in vitro research, which is better suited to deduce mechanisms of action.
Acute	Acute means sudden, sharp, and abrupt. Usually short in duration.
Lewin	Lewin ranks as one of the pioneers of social psychology, as one of the founders of group dynamics and as one of the most eminent representatives of Gestalt psychology.
Panic disorder with agoraphobia	In panic disorder with agoraphobia the person may experience severe panic attacks during situations where they feel trapped, insecure, out of control, or too far from their personal comfort zone. During severe bouts of anxiety, the person is confined not only to their home, but to one or two rooms and they may even become bedbound until their over-stimulated nervous system can quiet down, and their adrenaline levels return to a more normal level.
Response prevention	Response prevention is a behavior therapy technique in which the person is discouraged from making an accustomed response, used primarily with compulsive rituals.
Behavior rehearsal	A behavior therapy technique in which a client practices new behavior in the consulting room, often aided by demonstrations and role-play by the therapist is referred to as behavior rehearsal.
Stages	Stages represent relatively discrete periods of time in which functioning is qualitatively different from functioning at other periods.

Feedback Feedback refers to information returned to a person about the effects a response has had.

Obsession An obsession is a thought or idea that the sufferer cannot stop thinking about. Common examples include fears of acquiring disease, getting hurt, or causing harm to someone. They are typically automatic, frequent, distressing, and difficult to control or put an end to by themselves.

Habituation In habituation there is a progressive reduction in the response probability with continued repetition of a stimulus.

Assertiveness Assertiveness basically means the ability to express your thoughts and feelings in a way that clearly states your needs and keeps the lines of communication open with the other.

Assertiveness training In behavior therapy, a direct method of training people to express their own desires and feelings and to maintain their own rights in interactions with others, while at the same time respecting the others' rights is called assertiveness training.

Behavioral rehearsal Behavior therapy technique in which the client practices coping with troublesome or anxiety arousing situations in a safe and supervised situation is a behavioral rehearsal.

Contingency management Providing a supply of reinforcers to promote and maintain desired behaviors, and the prompt removal of reinforcers that maintain undesired behaviors is called contingency management.

Shaping The concept of reinforcing successive, increasingly accurate approximations to a target behavior is called shaping. The target behavior is broken down into a hierarchy of elemental steps, each step more sophisticated then the last. By successively reinforcing each of the the elemental steps, a form of differential reinforcement, until that step is learned while extinguishing the step below, the target behavior is gradually achieved.

Attention Attention is the cognitive process of selectively concentrating on one thing while ignoring other things. Psychologists have labeled three types of attention: sustained attention, selective attention, and divided attention.

Reinforcement contingencies The circumstances or rules that determine whether responses lead to the presentation of reinforcers are referred to as reinforcement contingencies. Skinner defined culture as a set of reinforcement contingencies.

Mental illness Mental illness is the term formerly used to mean psychological disorder but less preferred because it implies that the causes of the disorder can be found in a medical disease process.

Token economy An environmental setting that fosters desired behavior by reinforcing it with tokens that can be exchanged for other reinforcers is called a token economy.

Population Population refers to all members of a well-defined group of organisms, events, or things.

Chronic Chronic refers to a relatively long duration, usually more than a few months.

Mental retardation Mental retardation refers to having significantly below-average intellectual functioning and limitations in at least two areas of adaptive functioning. Many categorize retardation as mild, moderate, severe, or profound.

Social skills Social skills are skills used to interact and communicate with others to assist status in the social structure and other motivations.

Token economies Token economies is a technique used in behavioral therapy where subjects are given a token (that can be traded for something desirable) as a form of positive reinforcement for appropriate behavior.

Aversion therapy Aversion therapy is a now largely discredited form of treatment in which the patient is exposed to a stimulus while simultaneously being hurt or made ill. The theory is that the patient will come to associate the stimulus with unpleasant sensations and will no longer

seek it out.

Aversive stimulus A stimulus that elicits pain, fear, or avoidance is an aversive stimulus.

Habit strength Hull used the term habit to refer to an S-R association. Drive and habit act together to determine the habit strength. Thus the strength of behavior depends on both: the animal's motivation at time of testing, and the amount of prior learning. Hull referred to the concept as generalized habit strength.

Habit A habit is a response that has become completely separated from its eliciting stimulus. Early learning theorists used the term to describe S-R associations, however not all S-R associations become a habit, rather many are extinguished after reinforcement is withdrawn.

Temporal Contiguity Temporal contiguity occurs when two stimuli are experienced close together in time and, as a result an association may be formed. Superstitious behavior occurs as a result of the temporal contiguity between a behavior and a reinforcer/punisher that is independent of that behavior.

Punishment Punishment is the addtion of a stimulus that reduces the frequency of a response, or the removal of a stimulus that results in a reduction of the response.

Illumination Illumination is the physical, objective measurement of light falling on a surface.

Sensitization Sensitization is a process whereby an organism is made more responsive to certain aspects of its environment. For example, increases in the effects of a drug as a result of repeated administration. Also known as reverse tolerance.

Covert sensitization A form of aversion therapy in which the person is told to imagine undesirably attractive situations and activities while unpleasant feelings are being induced by imagery is covert sensitization.

Behavior modification Behavior Modification is a technique of altering an individual's reactions to stimuli through positive reinforcement and the extinction of maladaptive behavior.

Aversive conditioning A behavior therapy technique in which undesired responses are inhibited by pairing offensive stimuli with them is aversive conditioning.

Etiology Etiology is the study of causation. The term is used in philosophy, physics and biology in reference to the causes of various phenomena. It is generally the study of why things occur, or even the reasons behind the way that things act.

Beck Beck was initially trained as a psychoanalyst and conducted research on the psychoanalytic treatment of depression. With out the strong ability to collect data to this end, he began exploring cognitive approaches to treatment and originated cognitive behavior therapy.

Psychodynamic Most psychodynamic approaches are centered around the idea of a maladapted function developed early in life (usually childhood) which are at least in part unconscious. This maladapted function (a.k.a. defense mechanism) does not do well in place of a normal/healthy one.

Behaviorism The school of psychology that defines psychology as the study of observable behavior and studies relationships between stimuli and responses is called behaviorism. Behaviorism relied heavily on animal research and stated the same principles governed the behavior of both nonhumans and humans.

Depression In everyday language depression refers to any downturn in mood, which may be relatively transitory and perhaps due to something trivial. This is differentiated from Clinical depression which is marked by symptoms that last two weeks or more and are so severe that they interfere with daily living.

Radical Skinner defined behavior to include everything that an organism does, including thinking,

behaviorism	feeling and speaking and argued that these phenomena were valid subject matters of psychology. The term Radical Behaviorism refers to "everything an organism does is a behavior."
Social learning	Social learning is learning that occurs as a function of observing, retaining and replicating behavior observed in others. Although social learning can occur at any stage in life, it is thought to be particularly important during childhood, particularly as authority becomes important.
Social learning theory	Social learning theory explains the process of gender typing in terms of observation, imitation, and role playing .
Attitude	An enduring mental representation of a person, place, or thing that evokes an emotional response and related behavior is called attitude.
Vicarious learning	Vicarious learning is learning without specific reinforcement for one's behavior. It is learning by observing others.
Bandura	Bandura is best known for his work on social learning theory or Social Cognitivism. His famous Bobo doll experiment illustrated that people learn from observing others.
Affect	A subjective feeling or emotional tone often accompanied by bodily expressions noticeable to others is called affect.
Modeling	A type of behavior learned through observation of others demonstrating the same behavior is modeling.
Observational learning	The acquisition of knowledge and skills through the observation of others rather than by means of direct experience is observational learning. Four major processes are thought to influence the observational learning: attentional, retentional, behavioral production, and motivational.
Participant modeling	A behavior therapy in which an appropriate response is modeled in graduated steps and the client attempts each step, encouraged and supported by the therapist is participant modeling.
Masturbation	Masturbation is the manual excitation of the sexual organs, most often to the point of orgasm. It can refer to excitation either by oneself or by another, but commonly refers to such activities performed alone.
Script	A schema, or behavioral sequence, for an event is called a script. It is a form of schematic organization, with real-world events organized in terms of temporal and causal relations between component acts.
Incentive	An incentive is what is expected once a behavior is performed. An incentive acts as a reinforcer.
Coding	In senation, coding is the process by which information about the quality and quantity of a stimulus is preserved in the pattern of action potentials sent through sensory neurons to the central nervous system.
Albert Ellis	Albert Ellis is a psychologist whose Rational Emotive Behavior Therapy (REBT), is the foundation of all cognitive and cognitive behavior therapies.
Maladaptive	In psychology, a behavior or trait is adaptive when it helps an individual adjust and function well within their social environment. A maladaptive behavior or trait is counterproductive to the individual.
Wisdom	Wisdom is the ability to make correct judgments and decisions. It is an intangible quality gained through experience. Whether or not something is wise is determined in a pragmatic sense by its popularity, how long it has been around, and its ability to predict against future events.

Psychoanalytic
Freud's theory that unconscious forces act as determinants of personality is called psychoanalytic theory. The theory is a developmental theory characterized by critical stages of development.

Insight
Insight refers to a sudden awareness of the relationships among various elements that had previously appeared to be independent of one another.

Cognitive restructuring
Cognitive restructuring refers to any behavior therapy procedure that attempts to alter the manner in which a client thinks about life so that he or she changes overt behavior and emotions.

Trauma
Trauma refers to a severe physical injury or wound to the body caused by an external force, or a psychological shock having a lasting effect on mental life.

Rape
Rape is a crime where the victim is forced into sexual activity, in particular sexual penetration, against his or her will.

Stress inoculation
Use of positive coping statements to control fear and anxiety is a form of stress inoculation.

Cognitive therapy
Cognitive therapy is a kind of psychotherapy used to treat depression, anxiety disorders, phobias, and other forms of mental disorder. It involves recognizing distorted thinking and learning how to replace it with more realistic thoughts and actions.

Personality
Personality refers to the pattern of enduring characteristics that differentiates a person, the patterns of behaviors that make each individual unique.

Borderline personality disorder
Borderline personality disorder is characterized by extreme 'black and white' thinking, mood swings, emotional reasoning, disrupted relationships and difficulty in functioning in a way society accepts as normal.

Dialectical behavior therapy
Dialectical behavior therapy refers to a therapeutic approach to borderline personality disorder that combines client-centered empathy and acceptance with behavioral problem solving, social-skills training, and limit setting.

Personality disorder
A mental disorder characterized by a set of inflexible, maladaptive personality traits that keep a person from functioning properly in society is referred to as a personality disorder.

Emotional regulation
Techniques for controlling one's emotional states to efficiently adapt and reach a goal is called emotional regulation.

Emotion
An emotion is a mental states that arise spontaneously, rather than through conscious effort. They are often accompanied by physiological changes.

Relapse prevention
Extending therapeutic progress by teaching the client how to cope with future troubling situations is a relapse prevention technique.

Phenomenology
Phenomenology is the study of subjective mental experiences; a theme of humanistic theories of personality. It studies meaningful, intact mental events without dividing them for further analysis.

Clinical psychology
Clinical psychology is involved in the diagnosis, assessment, and treatment of patients with mental or behavioral disorders, and conducts research in these various areas.

Suicide
Suicide behavior is rare in childhood but escalates in adolescence. The suicide rate increases in a linear fashion from adolescence through late adulthood.

Problem solving
An attempt to find an appropriate way of attaining a goal when the goal is not readily available is called problem solving.

Pathology
Pathology is the study of the processes underlying disease and other forms of illness, harmful abnormality, or dysfunction.

Pragmatism	Pragmatism is characterized by the insistence on consequences, utility and practicality as vital components of truth. Pragmatism objects to the view that human concepts and intellect represent reality, and therefore stands in opposition to both formalist and rationalist schools of philosophy.
Paraprofessional	A paraprofessional is an individual lacking a doctoral degree but trained to perform certain functions usually reserved for clinicians.
Symptom substitution	Psychodynamic assertion that if overt problem behavior is treated without eliminating the underlying conflict thought to be causing it, that conflict will reemerge in the form of new, perhaps worse, symptoms is symptom substitution.
Socioeconomic	Socioeconomic pertains to the study of the social and economic impacts of any product or service offering, market intervention or other activity on an economy as a whole and on the companies, organization and individuals who are its main economic actors.
Behavioral tradition	Following the behavioral tradition, all that is needed to explain behavior is an observable and repeatable link between the behavior and the environment.
Bias	A bias is a prejudice in a general or specific sense, usually in the sense for having a preference to one particular point of view or ideological perspective.
Motives	Needs or desires that energize and direct behavior toward a goal are motives.
Humanistic	Humanistic refers to any system of thought focused on subjective experience and human problems and potentials.
Mental processes	The thoughts, feelings, and motives that each of us experiences privately but that cannot be observed directly are called mental processes.
Learning disability	A learning disability exists when there is a significant discrepancy between one's ability and achievement.
Comorbidity	Comorbidity refers to the presence of more than one mental disorder occurring in an individual at the same time.
Eating disorders	Psychological disorders characterized by distortion of the body image and gross disturbances in eating patterns are called eating disorders.
Bipolar disorder	Bipolar Disorder is a mood disorder typically characterized by fluctuations between manic and depressive states; and, more generally, atypical mood regulation and mood instability.
Substance abuse	Substance abuse refers to the overindulgence in and dependence on a stimulant, depressant, or other chemical substance, leading to effects that are detrimental to the individual's physical or mental health, or the welfare of others.
Schizophrenia	Schizophrenia is characterized by persistent defects in the perception or expression of reality. A person suffering from untreated schizophrenia typically demonstrates grossly disorganized thinking, and may also experience delusions or auditory hallucinations
Partial hospitalization	Partial hospitalization is a type of program used to treat mental illness and substance abuse. In partial hospitalization, the patient continues to reside at home, but commutes to a treatment center up to seven days a week. Since partial hospitalization focuses on the oversall treatment of the individual, rather than purely on his or her safety, the program is not used for people who are acutely suicidal.
Psychiatrist	A psychiatrist is a physician who specializes in the diagnosis and treatment of psychological disorders.
Counselor	A counselor is a mental health professional who specializes in helping people with problems not involving serious mental disorders.

Therapeutic alliance	A therapeutic alliance refers to a caring relationship that unites a therapist and a client in working to solve the client's problems.
Neuroscience	A field that combines the work of psychologists, biologists, biochemists, medical researchers, and others in the study of the structure and function of the nervous system is neuroscience.
Genetics	Genetics is the science of genes, heredity, and the variation of organisms.
Brain	The brain controls and coordinates most movement, behavior and homeostatic body functions such as heartbeat, blood pressure, fluid balance and body temperature. Functions of the brain are responsible for cognition, emotion, memory, motor learning and other sorts of learning. The brain is primarily made up of two types of cells: glia and neurons.
Theories	Theories are logically self-consistent models or frameworks describing the behavior of a certain natural or social phenomenon. They are broad explanations and predictions concerning phenomena of interest.
Premack principle	That any high-frequency response can be used to reinforce a low-frequency response is called the Premack Principle.
Reinforcer	In operant conditioning, a reinforcer is any stimulus that increases the probability that a preceding behavior will occur again. In Classical Conditioning, the unconditioned stimulus (US) is the reinforcer.
Positive reinforcer	In operant conditioning, a stimulus that is presented after a response that increases the likelihood that the response will be repeated is a positive reinforcer.

Group therapy

Group therapy is a form of psychotherapy during which one or several therapists treat a small group of clients together as a group. This may be more cost effective than individual therapy, and possibly even more effective.

Family therapy

Family therapy is a branch of psychotherapy that treats family problems. Family therapists consider the family as a system of interacting members; as such, the problems in the family are seen to arise as an emergent property of the interactions in the system, rather than ascribed exclusively to the "faults" or psychological problems of individual members.

Society

The social sciences use the term society to mean a group of people that form a semi-closed (or semi-open) social system, in which most interactions are with other individuals belonging to the group.

Couples therapy

Therapy with married or unmarried couples whose major problem is within their relationship is referred to as couples therapy.

Insight

Insight refers to a sudden awareness of the relationships among various elements that had previously appeared to be independent of one another.

Psychodrama

A therapy in which clients act out personal conflicts and feelings in the presence of others who play supporting roles is referred to as psychodrama.

Psychoanalyst

A psychoanalyst is a specially trained therapist who attempts to treat the individual by uncovering and revealing to the individual otherwise subconscious factors that are contributing to some undesirable behavor.

Psychoanalytic

Freud's theory that unconscious forces act as determinants of personality is called psychoanalytic theory. The theory is a developmental theory characterized by critical stages of development.

Pragmatism

Pragmatism is characterized by the insistence on consequences, utility and practicality as vital components of truth. Pragmatism objects to the view that human concepts and intellect represent reality, and therefore stands in opposition to both formalist and rationalist schools of philosophy.

Behavior therapy

Behavior therapy refers to the systematic application of the principles of learning to direct modification of a client's problem behaviors.

Gestalt therapy

Gestalt therapy is a form of psychotherapy, based on the experiential ideal of "here and now," and relationships with others and the world. By focusing the individual on their self-awareness as part of present reality, new insights can be made into their behavior, and they can engage in self-healing.

Free association

In psychoanalysis, the uncensored uttering of all thoughts that come to mind is called free association.

Psychotherapy

Psychotherapy is a set of techniques based on psychological principles intended to improve mental health, emotional or behavioral issues.

Transference

Transference is a phenomenon in psychology characterized by unconscious redirection of feelings from one person to another.

Anxiety

Anxiety is a complex combination of the feeling of fear, apprehension and worry often accompanied by physical sensations such as palpitations, chest pain and/or shortness of breath.

Attention

Attention is the cognitive process of selectively concentrating on one thing while ignoring other things. Psychologists have labeled three types of attention: sustained attention, selective attention, and divided attention.

Psychiatrist

A psychiatrist is a physician who specializes in the diagnosis and treatment of psychological

	disorders.
Learning	Learning is a relatively permanent change in behavior that results from experience. Thus, to attribute a behavioral change to learning, the change must be relatively permanent and must result from experience.
Motives	Needs or desires that energize and direct behavior toward a goal are motives.
Ego	In Freud's view the Ego serves to balance our primitive needs and our moral beliefs and taboos. Relying on experience, a healthy Ego provides the ability to adapt to reality and interact with the outside world.
Catharsis	Catharsis has been adopted by modern psychotherapy as the act of giving expression to deep emotions often associated with events in the individuals past which have never before been adequately expressed.
Social skills	Social skills are skills used to interact and communicate with others to assist status in the social structure and other motivations.
Guilt	Guilt describes many concepts related to a negative emotion or condition caused by actions which are believed to be, morally wrong. According to Freud, the avoidance of guilt is the basis for moral behavior.
Emotion	An emotion is a mental states that arise spontaneously, rather than through conscious effort. They are often accompanied by physiological changes.
Senses	The senses are systems that consist of a sensory cell type that respond to a specific kind of physical energy, and that correspond to a defined region within the brain where the signals are received and interpreted.
Desensitization	Desensitization refers to the type of sensory or behavioral adaptation in which we become less sensitive to constant stimuli.
Cognitive restructuring	Cognitive restructuring refers to any behavior therapy procedure that attempts to alter the manner in which a client thinks about life so that he or she changes overt behavior and emotions.
Assertiveness	Assertiveness basically means the ability to express your thoughts and feelings in a way that clearly states your needs and keeps the lines of communication open with the other.
Agoraphobia	An irrational fear of open, crowded places is called agoraphobia. Many people suffering from agoraphobia, however, are not afraid of the open spaces themselves, but of situations often associated with these spaces, such as social gatherings.
Depression	In everyday language depression refers to any downturn in mood, which may be relatively transitory and perhaps due to something trivial. This is differentiated from Clinical depression which is marked by symptoms that last two weeks or more and are so severe that they interfere with daily living.
Assertiveness training	In behavior therapy, a direct method of training people to express their own desires and feelings and to maintain their own rights in interactions with others, while at the same time respecting the others' rights is called assertiveness training.
Problem solving	An attempt to find an appropriate way of attaining a goal when the goal is not readily available is called problem solving.
Social phobia	An irrational, excessive fear of public scrutiny is referred to as social phobia.
Phobia	A persistent, irrational fear of an object, situation, or activity that the person feels compelled to avoid is referred to as a phobia.
In vivo	In vivo is used to indicate the presence of a whole/living organism, in distinction to a

	partial or dead organism, or a computer model. In vivo research is more suited to observe an overall effect than in vitro research, which is better suited to deduce mechanisms of action.
Stages	Stages represent relatively discrete periods of time in which functioning is qualitatively different from functioning at other periods.
Personality	Personality refers to the pattern of enduring characteristics that differentiates a person, the patterns of behaviors that make each individual unique.
Personality disorder	A mental disorder characterized by a set of inflexible, maladaptive personality traits that keep a person from functioning properly in society is referred to as a personality disorder.
Clinician	A health professional authorized to provide services to people suffering from one or more pathologies is a clinician.
Heterogeneous	A heterogeneous compound, mixture, or other such object is one that consists of many different items, which are often not easily sorted or separated, though they are clearly distinct.
Peer pressure	Peer pressure comprises a set of group dynamics whereby a group of people in which one feels comfortable may override the sexual personal habits, individual moral inhibitions or idiosyncratic desires to impose a group norm of attitudes or behaviors.
Affective	Affective is the way people react emotionally, their ability to feel another living thing's pain or joy.
Modeling	A type of behavior learned through observation of others demonstrating the same behavior is modeling.
Maladaptive	In psychology, a behavior or trait is adaptive when it helps an individual adjust and function well within their social environment. A maladaptive behavior or trait is counterproductive to the individual.
Eating disorders	Psychological disorders characterized by distortion of the body image and gross disturbances in eating patterns are called eating disorders.
Panic disorder	A panic attack is a period of intense fear or discomfort, typically with an abrupt onset and usually lasting no more than thirty minutes. The disorder is strikingly different from other types of anxiety, in that panic attacks are very sudden, appear to be unprovoked, and are often disabling. People who have repeated attacks, or feel severe anxiety about having another attack are said to have panic disorder.
Variable	A variable refers to a measurable factor, characteristic, or attribute of an individual or a system.
Psychological disorder	Mental processes and/or behavior patterns that cause emotional distress and/or substantial impairment in functioning is a psychological disorder.
Population	Population refers to all members of a well-defined group of organisms, events, or things.
Counselor	A counselor is a mental health professional who specializes in helping people with problems not involving serious mental disorders.
Clinical psychologist	A psychologist, usually with a Ph.D, whose training is in the diagnosis, treatment, or research of psychological and behavioral disorders is a clinical psychologist.
Clinical psychology	Clinical psychology is involved in the diagnosis, assessment, and treatment of patients with mental or behavioral disorders, and conducts research in these various areas.
Psychoanalysis	Psychoanalysis refers to the school of psychology that emphasizes the importance of unconscious motives and conflicts as determinants of human behavior. It was Freud's method of exploring human personality.

Humanism	Humanism refers to the philosophy and school of psychology that asserts that people are conscious, self-aware, and capable of free choice, self-fulfillment, and ethical behavior.
Behaviorism	The school of psychology that defines psychology as the study of observable behavior and studies relationships between stimuli and responses is called behaviorism. Behaviorism relied heavily on animal research and stated the same principles governed the behavior of both nonhumans and humans.
Schizophrenia	Schizophrenia is characterized by persistent defects in the perception or expression of reality. A person suffering from untreated schizophrenia typically demonstrates grossly disorganized thinking, and may also experience delusions or auditory hallucinations
Bateson	Bateson is most famous for developing the "Double Bind" theory of schizophrenia together with Paul Watzlawick.
Etiology	Etiology is the study of causation. The term is used in philosophy, physics and biology in reference to the causes of various phenomena. It is generally the study of why things occur, or even the reasons behind the way that things act.
Pathology	Pathology is the study of the processes underlying disease and other forms of illness, harmful abnormality, or dysfunction.
Intrapsychic conflict	In psychoanalysis, the struggles among the id, ego, and superego are an intrapsychic conflict.
Feedback	Feedback refers to information returned to a person about the effects a response has had.
Child development	Scientific study of the processes of change from conception through adolescence is called child development.
Counseling psychology	Counseling psychology is unique in its attention both to normal developmental issues and to problems associated with physical, emotional, and mental disorders.
Psychodynamic	Most psychodynamic approaches are centered around the idea of a maladapted function developed early in life (usually childhood) which are at least in part unconscious. This maladapted function (a.k.a. defense mechanism) does not do well in place of a normal/healthy one.
Presenting problem	The presenting problem is the original complaint reported by the client to the therapist. The actual treated problem may sometimes be a modification derived from the presenting problem or entirely different..
Empathy	Empathy is the recognition and understanding of the states of mind, including beliefs, desires and particularly emotions of others without injecting your own.
Direct instruction	Direct Instruction is a model for teaching that emphasizes well-developed and carefully planned lessons designed around small learning increments and clearly defined and prescribed teaching tasks. A criticism is that the approach turns children into passive learners and does not adequately challenge them to think in critical and creative ways.
Conjoint therapy	Therapy that sees couples, a family, or extended family at the same time is a conjoint therapy.
Reinforcement	In operant conditioning, reinforcement is any change in an environment that (a) occurs after the behavior, (b) seems to make that behavior re-occur more often in the future and (c) that reoccurence of behavior must be the result of the change.
Reinforcement contingencies	The circumstances or rules that determine whether responses lead to the presentation of reinforcers are referred to as reinforcement contingencies. Skinner defined culture as a set of reinforcement contingencies.
Sullivan	Sullivan developed the Self System, a configuration of the personality traits developed in

childhood and reinforced by positive affirmation and the security operations developed in childhood to avoid anxiety and threats to self-esteem.

Sex therapy — Sex therapy is the treatment of sexual dysfunction, such as non-consumation, premature ejaculation or erectile dysfunction, problems commonly caused by stress, tiredness and other environmental and relationship factors.

Empirical evidence — Facts or information based on direct observation or experience are referred to as empirical evidence.

Empirical — Empirical means the use of working hypotheses which are capable of being disproved using observation or experiment.

Effect size — An effect size is the strength or magnitude of the difference between two sets of data or, in outcome studies, between two time points for the same population. (The degree to which the null hypothesis is false).

Attachment — Attachment is the tendency to seek closeness to another person and feel secure when that person is present.

Humanistic — Humanistic refers to any system of thought focused on subjective experience and human problems and potentials.

Variability — Statistically, variability refers to how much the scores in a distribution spread out, away from the mean.

Therapeutic alliance — A therapeutic alliance refers to a caring relationship that unites a therapist and a client in working to solve the client's problems.

Family functioning — Family functioning is often defined in terms of the availability of two types of primary family resources: utilitarian and psychological.

Group dynamics — The term group dynamics implies that individual behaviors may differ depending on individuals' current or prospective connections to a sociological group.

Affect — A subjective feeling or emotional tone often accompanied by bodily expressions noticeable to others is called affect.

Brief therapy — A primary approach of brief therapy is to open up the present to admit a wider context and more appropriate understandings (not necessarily at a conscious level), rather than formal analysis of historical causes.

Valence — In expectancy theory, the value or worth a person gives to an outcome is called the valence.

Psychoanalysis	Psychoanalysis refers to the school of psychology that emphasizes the importance of unconscious motives and conflicts as determinants of human behavior. It was Freud's method of exploring human personality.
Insight	Insight refers to a sudden awareness of the relationships among various elements that had previously appeared to be independent of one another.
Clinical psychology	Clinical psychology is involved in the diagnosis, assessment, and treatment of patients with mental or behavioral disorders, and conducts research in these various areas.
Clinician	A health professional authorized to provide services to people suffering from one or more pathologies is a clinician.
Community psychology	Community psychology is the study of how to use the principles of psychology to create communities of all sizes that promote mental health of their members.
Ecology	Ecology refers to the branch of biology that deals with the relationships between living organisms and their environment.
Social norm	A social norm, is a rule that is socially enforced. In social situations, such as meetings, they are unwritten and often unstated rules that govern individuals' behavior. A social norm is most evident when not followed or broken.
Society	The social sciences use the term society to mean a group of people that form a semi-closed (or semi-open) social system, in which most interactions are with other individuals belonging to the group.
Syndrome	The term syndrome is the association of several clinically recognizable features, signs, symptoms, phenomena or characteristics which often occur together, so that the presence of one feature indicates the presence of the others.
Population	Population refers to all members of a well-defined group of organisms, events, or things.
Mental disorder	Mental disorder refers to a disturbance in a person's emotions, drives, thought processes, or behavior that involves serious and relatively prolonged distress and/or impairment in ability to function, is not simply a normal response to some event or set of events in the person's environment.
Premise	A premise is a statement presumed true within the context of a discourse, especially of a logical argument.
American Psychological Association	The American Psychological Association is a professional organization representing psychology in the US. The mission statement is to "advance psychology as a science and profession and as a means of promoting health, education , and human welfare".
Psychiatrist	A psychiatrist is a physician who specializes in the diagnosis and treatment of psychological disorders.
Clinical psychologist	A psychologist, usually with a Ph.D, whose training is in the diagnosis, treatment, or research of psychological and behavioral disorders is a clinical psychologist.
Psychotherapy	Psychotherapy is a set of techniques based on psychological principles intended to improve mental health, emotional or behavioral issues.
Mental illness	Mental illness is the term formerly used to mean psychological disorder but less preferred because it implies that the causes of the disorder can be found in a medical disease process.
Social class	Social class describes the relationships between people in hierarchical societies or cultures. Those with more power usually subordinate those with less power.
Antecedents	In behavior modification, events that typically precede the target response are called antecedents.

Autonomy	Autonomy is the condition of something that does not depend on anything else.
Discrimination	In Learning theory, discrimination refers the ability to distinguish between a conditioned stimulus and other stimuli. It can be brought about by extensive training or differential reinforcement. In social terms, it is the denial of privileges to a person or a group on the basis of prejudice.
Sexism	Sexism is commonly considered to be discrimination against people based on their sex rather than their individual merits, but can also refer to any and all differentiations based on
Consciousness	The awareness of the sensations, thoughts, and feelings being experienced at a given moment is called consciousness.
Microsystem	The setting or context in which an individual lives, including the person's family, peers, school, and neighborhood is a microsystem.
Affect	A subjective feeling or emotional tone often accompanied by bodily expressions noticeable to others is called affect.
Partial hospitalization	Partial hospitalization is a type of program used to treat mental illness and substance abuse. In partial hospitalization, the patient continues to reside at home, but commutes to a treatment center up to seven days a week. Since partial hospitalization focuses on the oversall treatment of the individual, rather than purely on his or her safety, the program is not used for people who are acutely suicidal.
Attitude	An enduring mental representation of a person, place, or thing that evokes an emotional response and related behavior is called attitude.
Emotion	An emotion is a mental states that arise spontaneously, rather than through conscious effort. They are often accompanied by physiological changes.
Depression	In everyday language depression refers to any downturn in mood, which may be relatively transitory and perhaps due to something trivial. This is differentiated from Clinical depression which is marked by symptoms that last two weeks or more and are so severe that they interfere with daily living.
Suicide	Suicide behavior is rare in childhood but escalates in adolescence. The suicide rate increases in a linear fashion from adolescence through late adulthood.
Social skills	Social skills are skills used to interact and communicate with others to assist status in the social structure and other motivations.
Schizophrenia	Schizophrenia is characterized by persistent defects in the perception or expression of reality. A person suffering from untreated schizophrenia typically demonstrates grossly disorganized thinking, and may also experience delusions or auditory hallucinations
Mental retardation	Mental retardation refers to having significantly below-average intellectual functioning and limitations in at least two areas of adaptive functioning. Many categorize retardation as mild, moderate, severe, or profound.
Attention	Attention is the cognitive process of selectively concentrating on one thing while ignoring other things. Psychologists have labeled three types of attention: sustained attention, selective attention, and divided attention.
Locus of control	The place to which an individual attributes control over the receiving of reinforcers -either inside or outside the self is referred to as locus of control.
Variable	A variable refers to a measurable factor, characteristic, or attribute of an individual or a system.
Norms	In testing, standards of test performance that permit the comparison of one person's score on

	the test to the scores of others who have taken the same test are referred to as norms.
Social identity	Social identity is the way we define ourselves in terms of group membership.
Ethnicity	Ethnicity refers to a characteristic based on cultural heritage, nationality characteristics, race, religion, and language.
Sexual orientation	Sexual orientation refers to the sex or gender of people who are the focus of a person's amorous or erotic desires, fantasies, and spontaneous feelings, the gender(s) toward which one is primarily "oriented".
Socioeconomic	Socioeconomic pertains to the study of the social and economic impacts of any product or service offering, market intervention or other activity on an economy as a whole and on the companies, organization and individuals who are its main economic actors.
Behavioral tradition	Following the behavioral tradition, all that is needed to explain behavior is an observable and repeatable link between the behavior and the environment.
Laboratory setting	Research setting in which the behavior of interest does not naturally occur is called a laboratory setting.
Behavior modification	Behavior Modification is a technique of altering an individual's reactions to stimuli through positive reinforcement and the extinction of maladaptive behavior.
Reinforcement	In operant conditioning, reinforcement is any change in an environment that (a) occurs after the behavior, (b) seems to make that behavior re-occur more often in the future and (c) that reoccurence of behavior must be the result of the change.
Job satisfaction	A person's attitudes and feelings about his or her job and facets of the job is called job satisfaction.
Alcoholism	A disorder that involves long-term, repeated, uncontrolled, compulsive, and excessive use of alcoholic beverages and that impairs the drinker's health and work and social relationships is called alcoholism.
Early childhood	Early childhood refers to the developmental period extending from the end of infancy to about 5 or 6 years of age; sometimes called the preschool years.
Deprivation	Deprivation, is the loss or withholding of normal stimulation, nutrition, comfort, love, and so forth; a condition of lacking. The level of stimulation is less than what is required.
Learning	Learning is a relatively permanent change in behavior that results from experience. Thus, to attribute a behavioral change to learning, the change must be relatively permanent and must result from experience.
Role model	A person who serves as a positive example of desirable behavior is referred to as a role model.
Paraprofessional	A paraprofessional is an individual lacking a doctoral degree but trained to perform certain functions usually reserved for clinicians.
Sympathetic	The sympathetic nervous system activates what is often termed the "fight or flight response". It is an automatic regulation system, that is, one that operates without the intervention of conscious thought.
Mentoring	Mentoring refers to a developmental relationship between a more experienced individual and a less experienced partner sometimes referred to as a protégé. In well-designed formal mentoring programs, there are program goals, schedules, and training.
Cultural diversity	Cultural diversity is the variety of human societies or cultures in a specific region, or in the world as a whole.

Epidemiology	Epidemiology is the study of the distribution and determinants of disease and disorders in human populations, and the use of its knowledge to control health problems.Epidemiology is considered the cornerstone methodology in all of public health research, and is highly regarded in evidence-based clinical medicine for identifying risk factors for disease and determining optimal treatment approaches to clinical practice.
Empirical	Empirical means the use of working hypotheses which are capable of being disproved using observation or experiment.
Psychopathology	Psychopathology refers to the field concerned with the nature and development of mental disorders.
Deinstitutio-alization	The transfer of former mental patients from institutions into the community is referred to as deinstitutionalization.
Adolescence	The period of life bounded by puberty and the assumption of adult responsibilities is adolescence.
Predisposition	Predisposition refers to an inclination or diathesis to respond in a certain way, either inborn or acquired. In abnormal psychology, it is a factor that lowers the ability to withstand stress and inclines the individual toward pathology.

Statistics — Statistics is a type of data analysis which practice includes the planning, summarizing, and interpreting of observations of a system possibly followed by predicting or forecasting of future events based on a mathematical model of the system being observed.

Statistic — A statistic is an observable random variable of a sample.

Chronic — Chronic refers to a relatively long duration, usually more than a few months.

Stroke — A stroke occurs when the blood supply to a part of the brain is suddenly interrupted by occlusion, by hemorrhage, or other causes

Health psychology — The field of psychology that studies the relationships between psychological factors and the prevention and treatment of physical illness is called health psychology.

Clinical psychology — Clinical psychology is involved in the diagnosis, assessment, and treatment of patients with mental or behavioral disorders, and conducts research in these various areas.

Behavioral medicine — Behavioral medicine refers to an interdisciplinary field that focuses on developing and integrating behavioral and biomedical knowledge to promote health and reduce illness.

Acupuncture — Whether acupuncture is efficacious or a placebo is subject to scientific research. Scientists have conducted reviews of existing clinical trials according to the protocols of evidence-based medicine; some have found efficacy for headache, low back pain and nausea, but for most conditions have concluded that there is insufficient evidence to determine whether or not acupuncture is effective.

Germ theory — The germ theory of disease is a theory that proposes that microorganisms are the cause of many diseases. Although highly controversial when first proposed, it is now a cornerstone of modern medicine.

Hippocrates — Hippocrates was an ancient Greek physician, commonly regarded as one of the most outstanding figures in medicine of all time; he has been called "the father of medicine."

Genetics — Genetics is the science of genes, heredity, and the variation of organisms.

Anatomy — Anatomy is the branch of biology that deals with the structure and organization of living things. It can be divided into animal anatomy (zootomy) and plant anatomy (phytonomy). Major branches of anatomy include comparative anatomy, histology, and human anatomy.

Generalization — In conditioning, the tendency for a conditioned response to be evoked by stimuli that are similar to the stimulus to which the response was conditioned is a generalization. The greater the similarity among the stimuli, the greater the probability of generalization.

Psychosomatic — A psychosomatic illness is one with physical manifestations and perhaps a supposed psychological cause. It is often diagnosed when any known or identifiable physical cause was excluded by medical examination.

Hypertension — Hypertension is a medical condition where the blood pressure in the arteries is chronically elevated. Persistent hypertension is one of the risk factors for strokes, heart attacks, heart failure and arterial aneurysm, and is a leading cause of chronic renal failure.

Asthma — Asthma is a complex disease characterized by bronchial hyperresponsiveness (BHR), inflammation, mucus production and intermittent airway obstruction.

Essential hypertension — Essential hypertension refers to a psychophysiological disorder characterized by high blood pressure that cannot be traced to an organic cause.

Empirical — Empirical means the use of working hypotheses which are capable of being disproved using observation or experiment.

Theories — Theories are logically self-consistent models or frameworks describing the behavior of a certain natural or social phenomenon. They are broad explanations and predictions concerning

phenomena of interest.

Psychiatrist A psychiatrist is a physician who specializes in the diagnosis and treatment of psychological disorders.

Obesity The state of being more than 20 percent above the average weight for a person of one's height is called obesity.

Attention Attention is the cognitive process of selectively concentrating on one thing while ignoring other things. Psychologists have labeled three types of attention: sustained attention, selective attention, and divided attention.

Cardiovascular disease Cardiovascular disease refers to afflictions in the mechanisms, including the heart, blood vessels, and their controllers, that are responsible for transporting blood to the body's tissues and organs. Psychological factors may play important roles in such diseases and their treatments.

Personality Personality refers to the pattern of enduring characteristics that differentiates a person, the patterns of behaviors that make each individual unique.

Affect A subjective feeling or emotional tone often accompanied by bodily expressions noticeable to others is called affect.

Trait An enduring personality characteristic that tends to lead to certain behaviors is called a trait. The term trait also means a genetically inherited feature of an organism.

Coronary heart disease Coronary heart disease is the end result of the accumulation of atheromatous plaques within the walls of the arteries that supply the myocardium (the muscle of the heart).

Type A personality Type A personality is a term used to describe people who are driven, hard-working, busy, and impatient. It was first described as an important risk factor in coronary disease in the 1950's by cardiologist Meyer Friedman and his co-workers.

Hypothesis A specific statement about behavior or mental processes that is testable through research is a hypothesis.

Behavioral risk factors Behaviors that increase the chances of disease, injury, or premature death are referred to as behavioral risk factors.

Biopsychosocial The biopsychosocial model is a way of looking at the mind and body of a patient as two important systems that are interlinked. The biopsychosocial model draws a distinction between the actual pathological processes that cause disease, and the patient's perception of their health and the effects on it, called the illness.

Social influence Social influence is when the actions or thoughts of individual(s) are changed by other individual(s). Peer pressure is an example of social influence.

Predisposition Predisposition refers to an inclination or diathesis to respond in a certain way, either inborn or acquired. In abnormal psychology, it is a factor that lowers the ability to withstand stress and inclines the individual toward pathology.

Cognition The intellectual processes through which information is obtained, transformed, stored, retrieved, and otherwise used is cognition.

Emotion An emotion is a mental states that arise spontaneously, rather than through conscious effort. They are often accompanied by physiological changes.

Immune system The most important function of the human immune system occurs at the cellular level of the blood and tissues. The lymphatic and blood circulation systems are highways for specialized white blood cells. These cells include B cells, T cells, natural killer cells, and macrophages. All function with the primary objective of recognizing, attacking and

	destroying bacteria, viruses, cancer cells, and all substances seen as foreign.
Transactional model	Transactional model refers to a framework that views development as the continuous and bidirectional interchange between an active organism with a unique biological constitution, and a changing environment.
Nervous system	The body's electrochemical communication circuitry, made up of billions of neurons is a nervous system.
Sympathetic	The sympathetic nervous system activates what is often termed the "fight or flight response". It is an automatic regulation system, that is, one that operates without the intervention of conscious thought.
Perception	Perception is the process of acquiring, interpreting, selecting, and organizing sensory information.
Adrenal medulla	Composed mainly of hormone-producing chromaffin cells, the adrenal medulla is the principal site of the conversion of the amino acid tyrosine into the catecholamines epinephrine and norepinephrine (also called adrenaline and noradrenaline, respectively).
Gland	A gland is an organ in an animal's body that synthesizes a substance for release such as hormones, often into the bloodstream or into cavities inside the body or its outer surface.
Pituitary gland	The pituitary gland is an endocrine gland about the size of a pea that sits in the small, bony cavity at the base of the brain. The pituitary gland secretes hormones regulating a wide variety of bodily activities, including trophic hormones that stimulate other endocrine glands.
Adrenal cortex	Adrenal cortex refers to the outer layer of the adrenal glands, which produces hormones that affect salt intake, reactions to stress, and sexual development.
Hypothalamus	The hypothalamus is a region of the brain located below the thalamus, forming the major portion of the ventral region of the diencephalon and functioning to regulate certain metabolic processes and other autonomic activities.
Forebrain	The forebrain is the highest level of the brain. Key structures in the forebrain are the limbic system, thalamus, basal ganglia, hypothalamus, and cerebral cortex.
Hormone	A hormone is a chemical messenger from one cell (or group of cells) to another. The best known are those produced by endocrine glands, but they are produced by nearly every organ system. The function of hormones is to serve as a signal to the target cells; the action of the hormone is determined by the pattern of secretion and the signal transduction of the receiving tissue.
Cortisol	Cortisol is a corticosteroid hormone that is involved in the response to stress; it increases blood pressure and blood sugar levels and suppresses the immune system. Synthetic cortisol, also known as hydrocortisone, is used as a drug mainly to fight allergies and inflammation.
Norepinephrine	Norepinephrine is released from the adrenal glands as a hormone into the blood, but it is also a neurotransmitter in the nervous system. As a stress hormone, it affects parts of the human brain where attention and impulsivity are controlled. Along with epinephrine, this compound effects the fight-or-flight response, activating the sympathetic nervous system to directly increase heart rate, release energy from fat, and increase muscle readiness.
Epinephrine	Epinephrine is a hormone and a neurotransmitter. Epinephrine plays a central role in the short-term stress reaction—the physiological response to threatening or exciting conditions. It is secreted by the adrenal medulla. When released into the bloodstream, epinephrine binds to multiple receptors and has numerous effects throughout the body.
Habit	A habit is a response that has become completely separated from its eliciting stimulus.

	Early learning theorists used the term to describe S-R associations, however not all S-R associations become a habit, rather many are extinguished after reinforcement is withdrawn.
Feedback loop	A system in which the hypothalamus, pituitary gland, and gonads regulate each other's functioning through a series of hormonal messages is a feedback loop.
Feedback	Feedback refers to information returned to a person about the effects a response has had.
Variable	A variable refers to a measurable factor, characteristic, or attribute of an individual or a system.
Social support	Social Support is the physical and emotional comfort given by family, friends, co-workers and others. Research has identified three main types of social support: emotional, practical, sharing points of view.
Syndrome	The term syndrome is the association of several clinically recognizable features, signs, symptoms, phenomena or characteristics which often occur together, so that the presence of one feature indicates the presence of the others.
Acquired immune deficiency syndrome	Acquired Immune Deficiency Syndrome is defined as a collection of symptoms and infections resulting from the depletion of the immune system caused by infection with the human immunodeficiency virus, commonly called HIV.
Human immunodefici-ncy virus	The human immunodeficiency virus is a retrovirus that primarily infects vital components of the human immune system. It is transmitted through penetrative and oral sex; blood transfusion; the sharing of contaminated needles in health care settings and through drug injection; and, between mother and infant, during pregnancy, childbirth and breastfeeding.
Population	Population refers to all members of a well-defined group of organisms, events, or things.
Primary caregiver	Primary caregiver refers to a person primarily responsible for the care of an infant, usually the infant's mother or father.
Eliciting Stimulus	An eliciting stimulus is a change in the environment that is highly correlated with the occurrence of a later response.
Neutral stimulus	A stimulus prior to conditioning that does not naturally result in the response of interest is called a neutral stimulus.
Stimulus	A change in an environmental condition that elicits a response is a stimulus.
Unconditioned stimulus	In classical conditioning, an unconditioned stimulus elicits a response from an organism prior to conditioning. It is a naturally occurring stimulus and a naturally occurring response..
Conditioned stimulus	A previously neutral stimulus that elicits the conditioned response because of being repeatedly paired with a stimulus that naturally elicited that response, is called a conditioned stimulus.
Desensitization	Desensitization refers to the type of sensory or behavioral adaptation in which we become less sensitive to constant stimuli.
Extinction	In operant extinction, if no reinforcement is delivered after the response, gradually the behavior will no longer occur in the presence of the stimulus. The process is more rapid following continuous reinforcement rather than after partial reinforcement. In Classical Conditioning, repeated presentations of the CS without being followed by the US results in the extinction of the CS.
Systematic desensitization	Systematic desensitization refers to Wolpe's behavioral fear-reduction technique in which a hierarchy of fear-evoking stimuli are presented while the person remains relaxed. The fear-evoking stimuli thereby become associated with muscle relaxation.

Anxiety	Anxiety is a complex combination of the feeling of fear, apprehension and worry often accompanied by physical sensations such as palpitations, chest pain and/or shortness of breath.
Countercondi-ioning	The process of eliminating a classically conditioned response by pairing the CS with an unconditioned stimulus for a response that is stronger than the conditioned response and that cannot occur at the same time as the CR is called counterconditioning.
Arousal	Arousal is a physiological and psychological state involving the activation of the reticular activating system in the brain stem, the autonomic nervous system and the endocrine system, leading to increased heart rate and blood pressure and a condition of alertness and readiness to respond.
Guided imagery	Guided imagery is the intentional visualization of images that are calming, relaxing, or beneficial in other ways .
Consciousness	The awareness of the sensations, thoughts, and feelings being experienced at a given moment is called consciousness.
Chemotherapy	Chemotherapy is the use of chemical substances to treat disease. In its modern-day use, it refers almost exclusively to cytostatic drugs used to treat cancer.In its non-oncological use, the term may also refer to antibiotics.
Conditioning	Conditioning describes the process by which behaviors can be learned or modified through interaction with the environment.
Operant Conditioning	A simple form of learning in which an organism learns to engage in behavior because it is reinforced is referred to as operant conditioning. The consequences of a behavior produce changes in the probability of the behavior's occurence.
Reinforcer	In operant conditioning, a reinforcer is any stimulus that increases the probability that a preceding behavior will occur again. In Classical Conditioning, the unconditioned stimulus (US) is the reinforcer.
Reinforcement	In operant conditioning, reinforcement is any change in an environment that (a) occurs after the behavior, (b) seems to make that behavior re-occur more often in the future and (c) that reoccurence of behavior must be the result of the change.
Stress inoculation	Use of positive coping statements to control fear and anxiety is a form of stress inoculation.
Sensation	Sensation is the first stage in the chain of biochemical and neurologic events that begins with the impinging of a stimulus upon the receptor cells of a sensory organ, which then leads to perception, the mental state that is reflected in statements like "I see a uniformly blue wall."
Maladaptive	In psychology, a behavior or trait is adaptive when it helps an individual adjust and function well within their social environment. A maladaptive behavior or trait is counterproductive to the individual.
Validity	The extent to which a test measures what it is intended to measure is called validity.
Biofeedback	Biofeedback is the process of measuring and quantifying an aspect of a subject's physiology, analyzing the data, and then feeding back the information to the subject in a form that allows the subject to enact physiological change.
Brain	The brain controls and coordinates most movement, behavior and homeostatic body functions such as heartbeat, blood pressure, fluid balance and body temperature. Functions of the brain are responsible for cognition, emotion, memory, motor learning and other sorts of learning. The brain is primarily made up of two types of cells: glia and neurons.

Tactile	Pertaining to the sense of touch is referred to as tactile.
Electrode	Any device used to electrically stimulate nerve tissue or to record its activity is an electrode.
Clinical study	An intensive investigation of a single person, especially one suffering from some injury or disease is referred to as a clinical study.
Placebo	Placebo refers to a bogus treatment that has the appearance of being genuine.
Substance abuse	Substance abuse refers to the overindulgence in and dependence on a stimulant, depressant, or other chemical substance, leading to effects that are detrimental to the individual's physical or mental health, or the welfare of others.
Personality trait	According to the Diagnostic and Statistical Manual of the American Psychiatric Association, a personality trait is a "prominent aspect of personality that is exhibited in a wide range of important social and personal contexts. ...".
Extraversion	Extraversion, one of the big-five personailty traits, is marked by pronounced engagement with the external world. They are people who enjoy being with people, are full of energy, and often experience positive emotions.
Addiction	Addiction is an uncontrollable compulsion to repeat a behavior regardless of its consequences. Many drugs or behaviors can precipitate a pattern of conditions recognized as addiction, which include a craving for more of the drug or behavior, increased physiological tolerance to exposure, and withdrawal symptoms in the absence of the stimulus.
Nicotine	Nicotine is an organic compound, an alkaloid found naturally throughout the tobacco plant, with a high concentration in the leaves. It is a potent nerve poison and is included in many insecticides. In lower concentrations, the substance is a stimulant and is one of the main factors leading to the pleasure and habit-forming qualities of tobacco smoking.
Cognitive therapy	Cognitive therapy is a kind of psychotherapy used to treat depression, anxiety disorders, phobias, and other forms of mental disorder. It involves recognizing distorted thinking and learning how to replace it with more realistic thoughts and actions.
Aversion therapy	Aversion therapy is a now largely discredited form of treatment in which the patient is exposed to a stimulus while simultaneously being hurt or made ill. The theory is that the patient will come to associate the stimulus with unpleasant sensations and will no longer seek it out.
Rapid smoking	Rapid smoking is a therapy technique in aversion therapy with prolonged smoking at a forced pace. It is used to produce discomfort for smoking.
Behavioral contract	A written agreement outlining a promise to adhere to the contingencies of a behavior modification program is a behavioral contract.
Social learning	Social learning is learning that occurs as a function of observing, retaining and replicating behavior observed in others. Although social learning can occur at any stage in life, it is thought to be particularly important during childhood, particularly as authority becomes important.
Role model	A person who serves as a positive example of desirable behavior is referred to as a role model.
Modeling	A type of behavior learned through observation of others demonstrating the same behavior is modeling.
Learning	Learning is a relatively permanent change in behavior that results from experience. Thus, to attribute a behavioral change to learning, the change must be relatively permanent and must result from experience.

Attitude	An enduring mental representation of a person, place, or thing that evokes an emotional response and related behavior is called attitude.
Alcoholism	A disorder that involves long-term, repeated, uncontrolled, compulsive, and excessive use of alcoholic beverages and that impairs the drinker's health and work and social relationships is called alcoholism.
Suicide	Suicide behavior is rare in childhood but escalates in adolescence. The suicide rate increases in a linear fashion from adolescence through late adulthood.
Liver	The liver plays a major role in metabolism and has a number of functions in the body including detoxification, glycogen storage and plasma protein synthesis. It also produces bile, which is important for digestion. The liver converts most carbohydrates, proteing, and fats into glucose.
Fetal alcohol syndrome	A cluster of abnormalities that appears in the offspring of mothers who drink alcohol heavily during pregnancy is called fetal alcohol syndrome.
Controlled drinking	A behavioral approach to the treatment of alcoholism, designed to teach the skills necessary so that alcoholics can drink socially without losing control is referred to as controlled drinking.
Relapse prevention	Extending therapeutic progress by teaching the client how to cope with future troubling situations is a relapse prevention technique.
Alcoholic	An alcoholic is dependent on alcohol as characterized by craving, loss of control, physical dependence and withdrawal symptoms, and tolerance.
Cerebral palsy	Cerebral palsy is a group of permanent disorders associated with developmental brain injuries that occur during fetal development, birth, or shortly after birth. It is characterized by a disruption of motor skills, with symptoms such as spasticity, paralysis, or seizures.
Counselor	A counselor is a mental health professional who specializes in helping people with problems not involving serious mental disorders.
Clinical psychologist	A psychologist, usually with a Ph.D, whose training is in the diagnosis, treatment, or research of psychological and behavioral disorders is a clinical psychologist.
Diabetes	Diabetes is a medical disorder characterized by varying or persistent elevated blood sugar levels, especially after eating. All types of diabetes share similar symptoms and complications at advanced stages: dehydration and ketoacidosis, cardiovascular disease, chronic renal failure, retinal damage which can lead to blindness, nerve damage which can lead to erectile dysfunction, gangrene with risk of amputation of toes, feet, and even legs.
Body mass index	The body mass index is a calculated number, used to compare and analyse the health effects of body weight on human bodies of all heights. It is equal to the weight, divided by the square of the height.
Gene	A gene is an ultramicroscopic area of the chromosome. It is the smallest physical unit of the DNA molecule that carries a piece of hereditary information.
Behavior modification	Behavior Modification is a technique of altering an individual's reactions to stimuli through positive reinforcement and the extinction of maladaptive behavior.
Early Intervention	Early intervention is a process used to recognize warning signs for mental health problems and to take early action against factors that put individuals at risk.
Positive reinforcement	In positive reinforcement, a stimulus is added and the rate of responding increases.
Gall	Gall most noted for introducing phrenology, was correct in assigning the brain the role of

	the seat of mental activities, and although he was wrong in detail due to a faulty methodology, the possibility of the localization of brain functions is widely accepted today.
Managed health care	A term that refers to the industrialization of health care, whereby large organizations in the private sector control the delivery of services is called managed health care.
Clinician	A health professional authorized to provide services to people suffering from one or more pathologies is a clinician.
Psychopharma-ology	Psychopharmacology refers to the study of the effects of drugs on the mind and on behavior; also known as medication and drug therapy.
Neuropsychology	Neuropsychology is a branch of psychology that aims to understand how the structure and function of the brain relates to specific psychological processes.
Psychoneuroi-munology	Psychoneuroimmunology is a specialist field of research that studies the connection between the brain, or mental states, and the immunal and hormonal systems of the human body.
Psychotherapy	Psychotherapy is a set of techniques based on psychological principles intended to improve mental health, emotional or behavioral issues.
Ethnicity	Ethnicity refers to a characteristic based on cultural heritage, nationality characteristics, race, religion, and language.
Biomedical model	The biomedical model has been around for centuries as the predominant model used by physicians in the diagnosis of disease. This model focuses on the physical processes, such as the pathology, the biochemistry and the physiology of a disease. It does not take into account the role of a person's mind or society in the cause and treatment.
Etiology	Etiology is the study of causation. The term is used in philosophy, physics and biology in reference to the causes of various phenomena. It is generally the study of why things occur, or even the reasons behind the way that things act.
Motivation	In psychology, motivation is the driving force (desire) behind all actions of an organism.
Conditioned response	A conditioned response is the response to a stimulus that occurs when an animal has learned to associate the stimulus with a certain positive or negative effect.

Brain	The brain controls and coordinates most movement, behavior and homeostatic body functions such as heartbeat, blood pressure, fluid balance and body temperature. Functions of the brain are responsible for cognition, emotion, memory, motor learning and other sorts of learning. The brain is primarily made up of two types of cells: glia and neurons.
Neuropsychology	Neuropsychology is a branch of psychology that aims to understand how the structure and function of the brain relates to specific psychological processes.
Clinical psychology	Clinical psychology is involved in the diagnosis, assessment, and treatment of patients with mental or behavioral disorders, and conducts research in these various areas.
Neuropsychol-gist	A psychologist concerned with the relationships among cognition, affect, behavior, and brain function is a neuropsychologist.
Neurologist	A physician who studies the nervous system, especially its structure, functions, and abnormalities is referred to as neurologist.
Standardized test	An oral or written assessment for which an individual receives a score indicating how the individual reponded relative to a previously tested large sample of others is referred to as a standardized test.
Lateralization	Lateralization refers to the dominance of one hemisphere of the brain for specific functions.
Lesion	A lesion is a non-specific term referring to abnormal tissue in the body. It can be caused by any disease process including trauma (physical, chemical, electrical), infection, neoplasm, metabolic and autoimmune.
Multiple sclerosis	Multiple sclerosis affects neurons, the cells of the brain and spinal cord that carry information, create thought and perception, and allow the brain to control the body. Surrounding and protecting these neurons is a layer of fat, called myelin, which helps neurons carry electrical signals. MS causes gradual destruction of myelin (demyelination) in patches throughout the brain and/or spinal cord, causing various symptoms depending upon which signals are interrupted.
Neuropsychol-gical test	A neuropsychological test use specifically designed tasks used to measure a psychological function known to be linked to a particular brain structure or pathway. They usually involve the systematic administration of clearly defined procedures in a formal environment.
Theories	Theories are logically self-consistent models or frameworks describing the behavior of a certain natural or social phenomenon. They are broad explanations and predictions concerning phenomena of interest.
Psychometric	Psychometric study is concerned with the theory and technique of psychological measurement, which includes the measurement of knowledge, abilities, attitudes, and personality traits. The field is primarily concerned with the study of differences between individuals
Health psychology	The field of psychology that studies the relationships between psychological factors and the prevention and treatment of physical illness is called health psychology.
Population	Population refers to all members of a well-defined group of organisms, events, or things.
Clinical psychologist	A psychologist, usually with a Ph.D, whose training is in the diagnosis, treatment, or research of psychological and behavioral disorders is a clinical psychologist.
Cardiovascular disease	Cardiovascular disease refers to afflictions in the mechanisms, including the heart, blood vessels, and their controllers, that are responsible for transporting blood to the body's tissues and organs. Psychological factors may play important roles in such diseases and their treatments.
Etiology	Etiology is the study of causation. The term is used in philosophy, physics and biology in reference to the causes of various phenomena. It is generally the study of why things occur,

or even the reasons behind the way that things act.

Phrenology — Phrenology is a theory which claims to be able to determine character, personality traits, and criminality on the basis of the shape of the head (reading "bumps"). Developed by Gall around 1800, and very popular in the 19th century, it is now discredited as a pseudoscience.

Gall — Gall most noted for introducing phrenology, was correct in assigning the brain the role of the seat of mental activities, and although he was wrong in detail due to a faulty methodology, the possibility of the localization of brain functions is widely accepted today.

Personality — Personality refers to the pattern of enduring characteristics that differentiates a person, the patterns of behaviors that make each individual unique.

Individual differences — Individual differences psychology studies the ways in which individual people differ in their behavior. This is distinguished from other aspects of psychology in that although psychology is ostensibly a study of individuals, modern psychologists invariably study groups.

Paul Broca — Paul Broca became famous with his discovery of the speech center, the third circumvolution of the frontal lobe. He arrived at this discovery by studying the brains of aphasic patients (persons unable to talk).

Pierre Flourens — Pierre Flourens pioneered the experimental method of carrying out localized lesions of the brain in living rabbits and pigeons and carefully observing their effects on motricity, sensibility and behavior. He was able to demonstrate convincingly for the first time that the main divisions of the brain were responsible for largely different functions.

Perception — Perception is the process of acquiring, interpreting, selecting, and organizing sensory information.

Arousal — Arousal is a physiological and psychological state involving the activation of the reticular activating system in the brain stem, the autonomic nervous system and the endocrine system, leading to increased heart rate and blood pressure and a condition of alertness and readiness to respond.

Psychological test — Psychological test refers to a standardized measure of a sample of a person's behavior.

Graham — Graham has conducted a number of studies that reveal stronger socioeconomic-status influences rather than ethnic influences in achievement.

Factor analysis — Factor analysis is a statistical technique that originated in psychometrics. The objective is to explain the most of the variability among a number of observable random variables in terms of a smaller number of unobservable random variables called factors.

Test battery — A group of tests and interviews given to the same individual is a test battery.

Left hemisphere — The left hemisphere of the cortex controls the right side of the body, coordinates complex movements, and, in 95% of people, controls the production of speech and written language.

Inference — Inference is the act or process of drawing a conclusion based solely on what one already knows.

Right hemisphere — The brain is divided into left and right cerebral hemispheres. The right hemisphere of the cortex controls the left side of the body.

Creativity — Creativity is the ability to think about something in novel and unusual ways and come up with unique solutions to problems. It involves divergent thinking, having many solutions or views to a problem.

Corpus callosum — The corpus callosum is the largest white matter structure in the brain. It consists of mostly of contralateral axon projections. The corpus callosum connects the left and right cerebral

	hemispheres. Most communication between regions in different halves of the brain are carried over the corpus callosum.
Occipital lobe	The occipital lobe is the smallest of four true lobes in the human brain. Located in the rearmost portion of the skull, the occipital lobe is part of the forebrain structure. It is the visual processing center.
Frontal lobe	The frontal lobe comprises four major folds of cortical tissue: the precentral gyrus, superior gyrus and the middle gyrus of the frontal gyri, the inferior frontal gyrus. It has been found to play a part in impulse control, judgement, language, memory, motor function, problem solving, sexual behavior, socialization and spontaneity.
Lobes	The four major sections of the cerebral cortex: frontal, parietal, temporal, and occipital are called lobes.
Cerebral hemisphere	Either of the two halves that make up the cerebrum is referred to as a cerebral hemisphere. The hemispheres operate together, linked by the corpus callosum, a very large bundle of nerve fibers, and also by other smaller commissures.
Temporal lobe	The temporal lobe is part of the cerebrum. It lies at the side of the brain, beneath the lateral or Sylvian fissure. Adjacent areas in the superior, posterior and lateral parts of the temporal lobe are involved in high-level auditory processing.
Parietal lobe	The parietal lobe is positioned above (superior to) the occipital lobe and behind (posterior to) the frontal lobe. It plays important roles in integrating sensory information from various senses, and in the manipulation of objects.
Tactile	Pertaining to the sense of touch is referred to as tactile.
Cerebellum	The cerebellum is located in the inferior posterior portion of the head (the hindbrain), directly dorsal to the brainstem and pons, inferior to the occipital lobe. The cerebellum is a region of the brain that plays an important role in the integration of sensory perception and fine motor output.
Cerebral cortex	The cerebral cortex is the outermost layer of the cerebrum and has a grey color. It is made up of four lobes and it is involved in many complex brain functions including memory, perceptual awareness, "thinking", language and consciousness. The cerebral cortex receives sensory information from many different sensory organs eg: eyes, ears, etc. and processes the information.
Lateral fissure	The lateral fissure is one of the most prominent structures of the human brain. It divides the frontal lobe and parietal lobe above from the temporal lobe below.
Trauma	Trauma refers to a severe physical injury or wound to the body caused by an external force, or a psychological shock having a lasting effect on mental life.
Concussion	Concussion, or mild traumatic brain injury (MTBI), is the most common and least serious type of brain injury. A milder type of diffuse axonal injury, concussion involves a transient loss of mental function. It can be caused by acceleration or deceleration forces, by a direct blow, or by penetrating injuries.
Contusion	Brain contusion, a form of traumatic brain injury, is a bruise of the brain tissue. Like bruises in other tissues, cerebral contusion can be caused by multiple microhemorrhages, small blood vessel leaks into brain tissue.
Delirium	Delirium is a medical term used to describe an acute decline in attention and cognition. Delirium is probably the single most common acute disorder affecting adults in general hospitals. It affects 10-20% of all adults in hospital, and 30-40% of older patients.
Stroke	A stroke occurs when the blood supply to a part of the brain is suddenly interrupted by

	occlusion, by hemorrhage, or other causes
Occlusion	The monocular depth cue occlusion is the blocking of sight of objects by other objects. It creates a "ranking" of nearness, and does not give any insight as to actual distances. In the absence of color or binocular vision, it often serves as the method of last resort for rudimentary depth perception.
Tumor	A tumor is an abnormal growth that when located in the brain can either be malignant and directly destroy brain tissue, or be benign and disrupt functioning by increasing intracranial pressure.
Affect	A subjective feeling or emotional tone often accompanied by bodily expressions noticeable to others is called affect.
Chorea	Chorea is the occurrence of continuous rapid, jerky, involuntary movements that may involve the face and limb and result in an inability to maintain a posture. It is also known as St. Vitus Dance disease and is seen mostly in children.
Malnutrition	Malnutrition is a general term for the medical condition in a person or animal caused by an unbalanced diet—either too little or too much food, or a diet missing one or more important nutrients.
Psychological disorder	Mental processes and/or behavior patterns that cause emotional distress and/or substantial impairment in functioning is a psychological disorder.
Consciousness	The awareness of the sensations, thoughts, and feelings being experienced at a given moment is called consciousness.
Chronic	Chronic refers to a relatively long duration, usually more than a few months.
Neurotransmitter	A neurotransmitter is a chemical that is used to relay, amplify and modulate electrical signals between a neurons and another cell.
Limbic system	The limbic system is a group of brain structures that are involved in various emotions such as aggression, fear, pleasure and also in the formation of memory. The limbic system affects the endocrine system and the autonomic nervous system. It consists of several subcortical structures located around the thalamus.
Emotional regulation	Techniques for controlling one's emotional states to efficiently adapt and reach a goal is called emotional regulation.
Alcoholic	An alcoholic is dependent on alcohol as characterized by craving, loss of control, physical dependence and withdrawal symptoms, and tolerance.
Mammillary body	The mammillary body is a pair of small round bodies in the brain forming part of the limbic system. Symptoms from damage to the mammillary bodies can include impaired memory, also called anterograde amnesia; this suggests that the mammillary bodies might be important for memory.
Hypothalamus	The hypothalamus is a region of the brain located below the thalamus, forming the major portion of the ventral region of the diencephalon and functioning to regulate certain metabolic processes and other autonomic activities.
Diencephalon	The diencephalon is the region of the brain that includes the epithalamus, thalamus, and hypothalamus. It is located above the mesencephalon of the brain stem. Sensory information is relayed between the brain stem and the rest of the brain regions
Mental disorder	Mental disorder refers to a disturbance in a person's emotions, drives, thought processes, or behavior that involves serious and relatively prolonged distress and/or impairment in ability to function, is not simply a normal response to some event or set of events in the person's environment.

Cingulate gyrus	Cingulate gyrus is a gyrus in the medial part of the brain. It partially wraps around the corpus callosum and is limited above by the cingulate sulcus. It functions as an intergral part of the limbic system, which is involved with emotion formation and processing, learning, and memory.
Hippocampus	The hippocampus is a part of the brain located inside the temporal lobe. It forms a part of the limbic system and plays a part in memory and navigation.
Spinal cord	The spinal cord is a part of the vertebrate nervous system that is enclosed in and protected by the vertebral column (it passes through the spinal canal). It consists of nerve cells. The spinal cord carries sensory signals and motor innervation to most of the skeletal muscles in the body.
Forebrain	The forebrain is the highest level of the brain. Key structures in the forebrain are the limbic system, thalamus, basal ganglia, hypothalamus, and cerebral cortex.
Thalamus	An area near the center of the brain involved in the relay of sensory information to the cortex and in the functions of sleep and attention is the thalamus.
Gyrus	A gyrus is a ridge on the cerebral cortex. It is generally surrounded by one or more sulci.
Labile	Easily emotionally moved, quickly shifting from one emotion to another, or easily aroused is referred to as labile.
Impulse control	Deferred gratification is the ability of a person to wait for things they want. This trait is critical for life success. Those who lack this trait are said to suffer from poor impulse control, and often become criminals, as they are unwilling to work and wait for their paycheck.
Apathy	Apathy is the lack of emotion, motivation, or enthusiasm. Apathy is a psychological term for a state of indifference — where an individual is unresponsive or "indifferent" to aspects of emotional, social, or physical life. Clinical apathy is considered to be at an elevated level, while a moderate level might be considered depression, and an extreme level could be diagnosed as a dissociative disorder.
Problem solving	An attempt to find an appropriate way of attaining a goal when the goal is not readily available is called problem solving.
Attitude	An enduring mental representation of a person, place, or thing that evokes an emotional response and related behavior is called attitude.
Visual perception	Visual perception is one of the senses, consisting of the ability to detect light and interpret it. Vision has a specific sensory system.
Attention	Attention is the cognitive process of selectively concentrating on one thing while ignoring other things. Psychologists have labeled three types of attention: sustained attention, selective attention, and divided attention.
Conceptual Behavior	Conceptual behavior is seen when an organism makes the same response to a group of discriminably different objects. An organism is said to respond conceptually when it responds similarly to stimuli within the same class and when it responds differently to stimuli in different classes.
Clinician	A health professional authorized to provide services to people suffering from one or more pathologies is a clinician.
Motivation	In psychology, motivation is the driving force (desire) behind all actions of an organism.
Psychosis	Psychosis is a generic term for mental states in which the components of rational thought and perception are severely impaired. Persons experiencing a psychosis may experience hallucinations, hold paranoid or delusional beliefs, demonstrate personality changes and

	exhibit disorganized thinking. This is usually accompanied by features such as a lack of insight into the unusual or bizarre nature of their behavior, difficulties with social interaction and impairments in carrying out the activities of daily living.
Empirical evidence	Facts or information based on direct observation or experience are referred to as empirical evidence.
Empirical	Empirical means the use of working hypotheses which are capable of being disproved using observation or experiment.
Premorbid	Premorbid refers to individual's level of functioning prior to the development of a disorder.
Validity	The extent to which a test measures what it is intended to measure is called validity.
Hypothesis	A specific statement about behavior or mental processes that is testable through research is a hypothesis.
Variability	Statistically, variability refers to how much the scores in a distribution spread out, away from the mean.
Photon	A photon is a quantum of the electromagnetic field, for instance light. In some respects a photon acts as a particle, for instance when registered by the light sensitive device in a camera. It also acts like a wave, as when passing through the optics in a camera.
Single photon emission computed tomography	Single photon emission computed tomography uses gamma ray emitting radioisotopes and a gamma camera to record data that a computer uses to construct two- or three-dimensional images of active brain regions.
Computed tomography	Computed tomography is an imaging method employing tomography where digital processing is used to generate a three-dimensional image of the internals of an object from a large series of two-dimensional X-ray images taken around a single axis of rotation.
Reasoning	Reasoning is the act of using reason to derive a conclusion from certain premises. There are two main methods to reach a conclusion,deductive reasoning and inductive reasoning.
Stimulus	A change in an environmental condition that elicits a response is a stimulus.
Feedback	Feedback refers to information returned to a person about the effects a response has had.
Wechsler	Wechsler is best known for his intelligence tests. The Wechsler Adult Intelligence Scale (WAIS) was developed first in 1939 and then called the Wechsler-Bellevue Intelligence Test. From these he derived the Wechsler Intelligence Scale for Children (WISC) in 1949 and the Wechsler Preschool and Primary Scale of Intelligence (WPPSI) in 1967. Wechsler originally created these tests to find out more about his patients at the Bellevue clinic and he found the then-current Binet IQ test unsatisfactory.
Working Memory	Working memory is the collection of structures and processes in the brain used for temporarily storing and manipulating information. Working memory consists of both memory for items that are currently being processed, and components governing attention and directing the processing itself.
Normative	The term normative is used to describe the effects of those structures of culture which regulate the function of social activity.
Aphasia	Aphasia is a loss or impairment of the ability to produce or comprehend language, due to brain damage. It is usually a result of damage to the language centers of the brain.
Psychological deficit	The term used to indicate that performance of a pertinent psychological process is below that expected of a normal person is psychological deficit.
Reliability	Reliability means the extent to which a test produces a consistent , reproducible score .

Depression	In everyday language depression refers to any downturn in mood, which may be relatively transitory and perhaps due to something trivial. This is differentiated from Clinical depression which is marked by symptoms that last two weeks or more and are so severe that they interfere with daily living.
Variable	A variable refers to a measurable factor, characteristic, or attribute of an individual or a system.
Norms	In testing, standards of test performance that permit the comparison of one person's score on the test to the scores of others who have taken the same test are referred to as norms.
Brain trauma	Brain Trauma, also called acquired brain injury, intracranial injury, or simply head injury, occurs when a sudden trauma causes damage to the brain.
Handedness	A preference for the right or left hand in most activities is referred to as handedness. Right-handedness is dominant in all cultures, and it appears before culture can influence the child.
Malingering	Malingering is a medical and psychological term that refers to an individual faking the symptoms of mental or physical disorders for a myriad of reasons such as fraud, dereliction of responsibilities, attempting to obtain medications or to lighten criminal sentences.
Spontaneous recovery	The recurrence of an extinguished response as a function of the passage of time is referred to as spontaneous recovery.
American Psychological Association	The American Psychological Association is a professional organization representing psychology in the US. The mission statement is to "advance psychology as a science and profession and as a means of promoting health, education , and human welfare".
Social psychology	Social psychology is the study of the nature and causes of human social behavior, with an emphasis on how people think towards each other and how they relate to each other.
Research design	A research design tests a hypothesis. The basic typess are: descriptive, correlational, and experimental.
Neurochemistry	Neurochemistry is a branch of neuroscience that is heavily devoted to the study of neurochemicals. A neurochemical is an organic molecule that participates in neural activity. This term is often used to refer to neurotransmitters and other molecules such as neuro-active drugs that influence neuron function.
Knowledge base	The general background information a person possesses, which influences most cognitive task performance is called the knowledge base.
Neuroanatomy	Neuroanatomy is the study of the anatomy of the central nervous system.
Neuroscience	A field that combines the work of psychologists, biologists, biochemists, medical researchers, and others in the study of the structure and function of the nervous system is neuroscience.
Statistics	Statistics is a type of data analysis which practice includes the planning, summarizing, and interpreting of observations of a system possibly followed by predicting or forecasting of future events based on a mathematical model of the system being observed.
Statistic	A statistic is an observable random variable of a sample.
Learning	Learning is a relatively permanent change in behavior that results from experience. Thus, to attribute a behavioral change to learning, the change must be relatively permanent and must result from experience.
Physiological psychology	Physiological psychology refers to the study of the physiological mechanisms, in the brain and elsewhere, that mediate behavior and psychological experiences.

Developmental psychology	The branch of psychology that studies the patterns of growth and change occurring throughout life is referred to as developmental psychology.
Executive function	The processes involved in regulating attention and in determining what to do with information just gathered or retrieved from long-term memory, is referred to as the executive function.
Prognosis	A forecast about the probable course of an illess is referred to as prognosis.
Localization of function	Localization of function is the concept that different parts of the brain serve different, specifiable functions in the control of mental experience and behavior.
Traumatic brain injury	Traumatic brain injury, also called acquired brain injury, intracranial injury, or simply head injury, occurs when a sudden trauma causes damage to the brain.
Neuroimaging	Neuroimaging comprises all invasive, minimally invasive, and non-invasive methods for obtaing structural and functional images of the nervous system's major subsystems: the brain, the peripheral nervous system, and the spinal cord.
Cognition	The intellectual processes through which information is obtained, transformed, stored, retrieved, and otherwise used is cognition.
Agnosia	Agnosia is a loss of ability to recognize objects, persons, sounds, shapes or smells while the specific sense is not defective nor is there any significant memory loss.
Apraxia	Apraxia is a neurological disorder characterized by loss of the ability to execute or carry out learned movements, despite having the desire and the physical ability to perform the movements.
Cerebral hemorrhage	Cerebral hemorrhage is a form of stroke that occurs when a blood vessel in the brain ruptures or bleeds. Hemorrhagic strokes are deadlier than their more common counterpart, ischemic strokes.
Nervous system	The body's electrochemical communication circuitry, made up of billions of neurons is a nervous system.
Neuron	The neuron is the primary cell of the nervous system. They are found in the brain, the spinal cord, in the nerves and ganglia of the peripheral nervous system. It is a specialized cell that conducts impulses through the nervous system and contains three major parts: cell body, dendrites, and an axon. It can have many dendrites but only one axon.
Central nervous system	The vertebrate central nervous system consists of the brain and spinal cord.
Emotion	An emotion is a mental states that arise spontaneously, rather than through conscious effort. They are often accompanied by physiological changes.
Pathognomonic	Pathognomonic is a word, often used in medicine, which means characteristic or diagnostic for a particular disease.

Munsterberg	Munsterberg was a pioneer in industrial psychology, and held controversial views on the reliability of witness testimony.
Wundt	Wundt, considered the father of experimental psychology, created the first laboratory in psychology in 1879. His methodology was based on introspection and his body of work founded the school of thought called Voluntarism.
Psychiatrist	A psychiatrist is a physician who specializes in the diagnosis and treatment of psychological disorders.
William Stern	William Stern developed the original formula for the Intelligence Quotient (IQ) after studying the scores on Binet's intelligence test.
Watson	Watson, the father of behaviorism, developed the term "Behaviorism" as a name for his proposal to revolutionize the study of human psychology in order to put it on a firm experimental footing.
Empirical	Empirical means the use of working hypotheses which are capable of being disproved using observation or experiment.
Terman	Terman revised the Stanford-Binet Intelligence Scale in 1916, commonly used to measure intelligence (or I.Q.) in the United States. William Stern's suggestion that mental age/chronological age times 100 (to get rid of the decimal) be made the "intelligence quotient" or I.Q. This apparent mathematization of the measurement gave it an air of scientific accuracy and detachment which contributed greatly to its acceptance among educators and the broad public.
Forensic psychology	Psychological research and theory that deals with the effects of cognitive, affective, and behavioral factors on legal proceedings and the law is a forensic psychology.
Survey	A method of scientific investigation in which a large sample of people answer questions about their attitudes or behavior is referred to as a survey.
Clinical psychologist	A psychologist, usually with a Ph.D, whose training is in the diagnosis, treatment, or research of psychological and behavioral disorders is a clinical psychologist.
Clinical psychology	Clinical psychology is involved in the diagnosis, assessment, and treatment of patients with mental or behavioral disorders, and conducts research in these various areas.
Society	The social sciences use the term society to mean a group of people that form a semi-closed (or semi-open) social system, in which most interactions are with other individuals belonging to the group.
American Psychological Association	The American Psychological Association is a professional organization representing psychology in the US. The mission statement is to "advance psychology as a science and profession and as a means of promoting health, education , and human welfare".
Compensation	In personaility, compensation, according to Adler, is an effort to overcome imagined or real inferiorities by developing one's abilities.
Sexual harassment	Deliberate or repeated verbal comments, gestures, or physical contact of a sexual nature that is unwanted by the recipient is called sexual harassment.
Inference	Inference is the act or process of drawing a conclusion based solely on what one already knows.
Learning	Learning is a relatively permanent change in behavior that results from experience. Thus, to attribute a behavioral change to learning, the change must be relatively permanent and must result from experience.
Validity	The extent to which a test measures what it is intended to measure is called validity.

Anxiety	Anxiety is a complex combination of the feeling of fear, apprehension and worry often accompanied by physical sensations such as palpitations, chest pain and/or shortness of breath.
Neuropsychologist	A psychologist concerned with the relationships among cognition, affect, behavior, and brain function is a neuropsychologist.
Insanity	A legal status indicating that a person cannot be held responsible for his or her actions because of mental illness is called insanity.
Insanity defense	In a criminal trial, the insanity defense is a possible defense by excuse, via which defendants may argue that they should not be held criminally liable for breaking the law, as they were mentally ill or mentally incompetent at the time of their allegedly "criminal" actions.
Durham standard	A test of legal insanity known as the products rest-an accused person is not responsible if the unlawful act was the product of mental disease or defect is a Durham standard.
Perception	Perception is the process of acquiring, interpreting, selecting, and organizing sensory information.
Brazelton	Brazelton Neonatal Behavioral Assessment Scale is a test given several days after birth to assess newborns' neurological development, reflexes, and reactions to people.
Mental illness	Mental illness is the term formerly used to mean psychological disorder but less preferred because it implies that the causes of the disorder can be found in a medical disease process.
Mental disorder	Mental disorder refers to a disturbance in a person's emotions, drives, thought processes, or behavior that involves serious and relatively prolonged distress and/or impairment in ability to function, is not simply a normal response to some event or set of events in the person's environment.
Personality	Personality refers to the pattern of enduring characteristics that differentiates a person, the patterns of behaviors that make each individual unique.
Malingering	Malingering is a medical and psychological term that refers to an individual faking the symptoms of mental or physical disorders for a myriad of reasons such as fraud, dereliction of responsibilities, attempting to obtain medications or to lighten criminal sentences.
Attention	Attention is the cognitive process of selectively concentrating on one thing while ignoring other things. Psychologists have labeled three types of attention: sustained attention, selective attention, and divided attention.
Involuntary commitment	Involuntary commitment is the practice of using legal means or forms as part of a mental health law to commit a person to a mental hospital, insane asylum or psychiatric ward against their will or over their protests. Many but not all countries have mental health laws governing involuntary commitment.
Hallucination	A hallucination is a sensory perception experienced in the absence of an external stimulus, as distinct from an illusion, which is a misperception of an external stimulus. They may occur in any sensory modality - visual, auditory, olfactory, gustatory, tactile, or mixed.
Delusion	A false belief, not generally shared by others, and that cannot be changed despite strong evidence to the contrary is a delusion.
Child abuse	Child abuse is the physical or psychological maltreatment of a child.
Norms	In testing, standards of test performance that permit the comparison of one person's score on the test to the scores of others who have taken the same test are referred to as norms.
Right to refuse	A legal principle according to which a committed mental patient may decline to participate in

treatment	treatment is the right to refuse treatment.
Clinician	A health professional authorized to provide services to people suffering from one or more pathologies is a clinician.
Empirical evidence	Facts or information based on direct observation or experience are referred to as empirical evidence.
Deprivation	Deprivation, is the loss or withholding of normal stimulation, nutrition, comfort, love, and so forth; a condition of lacking. The level of stimulation is less than what is required.
Punishment	Punishment is the addtion of a stimulus that reduces the frequency of a response, or the removal of a stimulus that results in a reduction of the response.
Behavior modification	Behavior Modification is a technique of altering an individual's reactions to stimuli through positive reinforcement and the extinction of maladaptive behavior.
Cognitive approach	A cognitive approach focuses on the mental processes involved in knowing: how we direct our attention, perceive, remember, think, and solve problems.
Biofeedback	Biofeedback is the process of measuring and quantifying an aspect of a subject's physiology, analyzing the data, and then feeding back the information to the subject in a form that allows the subject to enact physiological change.
Insight	Insight refers to a sudden awareness of the relationships among various elements that had previously appeared to be independent of one another.
Questionnaire	A self-report method of data collection or clinical assessment method in which the individual being studied checks off items on a printed list, answers multiple-choice questions, or writes out answers to essay questions aimed at producing a selfdescription is called questionnaire.
Simulation	A simulation is an imitation of some real device or state of affairs. Simulation attempts to represent certain features of the behavior of a physical or abstract system by the behavior of another system.
Bias	A bias is a prejudice in a general or specific sense, usually in the sense for having a preference to one particular point of view or ideological perspective.
Representative sample	Representative sample refers to a sample of participants selected from the larger population in such a way that important subgroups within the population are included in the sample in the same proportions as they are found in the larger population.
Attitude	An enduring mental representation of a person, place, or thing that evokes an emotional response and related behavior is called attitude.
Emotion	An emotion is a mental states that arise spontaneously, rather than through conscious effort. They are often accompanied by physiological changes.
Prejudice	Prejudice in general, implies coming to a judgment on the subject before learning where the preponderance of the evidence actually lies, or formation of a judgement without direct experience.
Loftus	Loftus works on human memory and how it can be changed by facts, ideas, suggestions and other forms of post-event information. One of her famous studies include the "car accident" study, which was an example of the misinformation effect.
Feedback	Feedback refers to information returned to a person about the effects a response has had.
Affect	A subjective feeling or emotional tone often accompanied by bodily expressions noticeable to others is called affect.

Elaboration	The extensiveness of processing at any given level of memory is called elaboration. The use of elaboration changes developmentally. Adolescents are more likely to use elaboration spontaneously than children.
Shadowing	A monocular cue for depth based on the fact that opaque objects block light and produce shadows is called shadowing.

Population	Population refers to all members of a well-defined group of organisms, events, or things.
Projection	Attributing one's own undesirable thoughts, impulses, traits, or behaviors to others is referred to as projection.
Clinical psychology	Clinical psychology is involved in the diagnosis, assessment, and treatment of patients with mental or behavioral disorders, and conducts research in these various areas.
Clinician	A health professional authorized to provide services to people suffering from one or more pathologies is a clinician.
Psychodynamic	Most psychodynamic approaches are centered around the idea of a maladapted function developed early in life (usually childhood) which are at least in part unconscious. This maladapted function (a.k.a. defense mechanism) does not do well in place of a normal/healthy one.
Family therapy	Family therapy is a branch of psychotherapy that treats family problems. Family therapists consider the family as a system of interacting members; as such, the problems in the family are seen to arise as an emergent property of the interactions in the system, rather than ascribed exclusively to the "faults" or psychological problems of individual members.
Survey	A method of scientific investigation in which a large sample of people answer questions about their attitudes or behavior is referred to as a survey.
Witmer	Witmer first described and coined the terms clinical psychology and psychological clinic. In the beginning of clinical psychology, pioneers such as Witmer saw the benefit of a collaboration between mental health and medical health care provision.
Psychoanalysis	Psychoanalysis refers to the school of psychology that emphasizes the importance of unconscious motives and conflicts as determinants of human behavior. It was Freud's method of exploring human personality.
Behaviorism	The school of psychology that defines psychology as the study of observable behavior and studies relationships between stimuli and responses is called behaviorism. Behaviorism relied heavily on animal research and stated the same principles governed the behavior of both nonhumans and humans.
Mental retardation	Mental retardation refers to having significantly below-average intellectual functioning and limitations in at least two areas of adaptive functioning. Many categorize retardation as mild, moderate, severe, or profound.
Society	The social sciences use the term society to mean a group of people that form a semi-closed (or semi-open) social system, in which most interactions are with other individuals belonging to the group.
Conduct disorder	Conduct disorder is the psychiatric diagnostic category for the occurrence of multiple delinquent activities over a 6-month period. These behaviors include truancy, running away, fire setting, cruelty to animals, breaking and entering, and excessive fighting.
Hyperactivity	Hyperactivity can be described as a state in which a individual is abnormally easily excitable and exuberant. Strong emotional reactions and a very short span of attention is also typical for the individual.
Mental disorder	Mental disorder refers to a disturbance in a person's emotions, drives, thought processes, or behavior that involves serious and relatively prolonged distress and/or impairment in ability to function, is not simply a normal response to some event or set of events in the person's environment.
Resilient children	Resilient children weather adverse circumstances, function well despite challenges or threats, or bounce back from traumatic events.
Autistic	An autistic disorder is a neurodevelopmental disorder that manifests itself in markedly

disorder	abnormal social interaction, communication ability, patterns of interests, and patterns of behavior.
Personal identity	The portion of the self-concept that pertains to the self as a distinct, separate individual is called personal identity.
Learning disorder	A disorder characterized by a discrepancy between one's academic achievement and one's intellectual ability is referred to as a learning disorder.
Anxiety disorder	Anxiety disorder is a blanket term covering several different forms of abnormal anxiety, fear, phobia and nervous condition, that come on suddenly and prevent pursuing normal daily routines.
Schizophrenia	Schizophrenia is characterized by persistent defects in the perception or expression of reality. A person suffering from untreated schizophrenia typically demonstrates grossly disorganized thinking, and may also experience delusions or auditory hallucinations
School phobia	An acute, irrational dread of attending school, usually accompanied by somatic complaints is called school phobia.
Depression	In everyday language depression refers to any downturn in mood, which may be relatively transitory and perhaps due to something trivial. This is differentiated from Clinical depression which is marked by symptoms that last two weeks or more and are so severe that they interfere with daily living.
Learning	Learning is a relatively permanent change in behavior that results from experience. Thus, to attribute a behavioral change to learning, the change must be relatively permanent and must result from experience.
Suicide	Suicide behavior is rare in childhood but escalates in adolescence. The suicide rate increases in a linear fashion from adolescence through late adulthood.
Anxiety	Anxiety is a complex combination of the feeling of fear, apprehension and worry often accompanied by physical sensations such as palpitations, chest pain and/or shortness of breath.
Bulimia	Bulimia refers to a disorder in which a person binges on incredibly large quantities of food, then purges by vomiting or by using laxatives. Bulimia is often less about food, and more to do with deep psychological issues and profound feelings of lack of control.
Phobia	A persistent, irrational fear of an object, situation, or activity that the person feels compelled to avoid is referred to as a phobia.
Authoritative parenting	Authoritative parenting encourages children to be independent but still places limits and controls on their actions. Extensive verbal give-and-take is allowed, and parents are warm and nurturant toward the child.
Psychopathology	Psychopathology refers to the field concerned with the nature and development of mental disorders.
Perception	Perception is the process of acquiring, interpreting, selecting, and organizing sensory information.
Adolescence	The period of life bounded by puberty and the assumption of adult responsibilities is adolescence.
Infancy	The developmental period that extends from birth to 18 or 24 months is called infancy.
Shyness	A tendency to avoid others plus uneasiness and strain when socializing is called shyness.
Achievement test	A test designed to determine a person's level of knowledge in a given subject area is referred to as an achievement test.

Neuropsychological test — A neuropsychological test use specifically designed tasks used to measure a psychological function known to be linked to a particular brain structure or pathway. They usually involve the systematic administration of clearly defined procedures in a formal environment.

Emotion — An emotion is a mental states that arise spontaneously, rather than through conscious effort. They are often accompanied by physiological changes.

Direct observation — Direct observation refers to assessing behavior through direct surveillance.

Coding — In senation, coding is the process by which information about the quality and quantity of a stimulus is preserved in the pattern of action potentials sent through sensory neurons to the central nervous system.

Reid — Reid was the founder of the Scottish School of Common Sense, and played an integral role in the Scottish Enlightenment. He advocated direct realism, or common sense realism, and argued strongly against the Theory of Ideas advocated by John Locke and René Descartes.

Intelligence test — An intelligence test is a standardized means of assessing a person's current mental ability, for example, the Stanford-Binet test and the Wechsler Adult Intelligence Scale.

Working Memory — Working memory is the collection of structures and processes in the brain used for temporarily storing and manipulating information. Working memory consists of both memory for items that are currently being processed, and components governing attention and directing the processing itself.

Reasoning — Reasoning is the act of using reason to derive a conclusion from certain premises. There are two main methods to reach a conclusion,deductive reasoning and inductive reasoning.

Learning disability — A learning disability exists when there is a significant discrepancy between one's ability and achievement.

Test battery — A group of tests and interviews given to the same individual is a test battery.

Projective test — A projective test is a personality test designed to let a person respond to ambiguous stimuli, presumably revealing hidden emotions and internal conflicts. This is different from an "objective test" in which responses are analyzed according to a universal standard rather than an individual psychiatrist's judgement.

Reliability — Reliability means the extent to which a test produces a consistent , reproducible score .

Validity — The extent to which a test measures what it is intended to measure is called validity.

Apperception — A newly experienced sensation is related to past experiences to form an understood situation. For Wundt, consciousness is composed of two "stages:" There is a large capacity working memory called the Blickfeld and the narrower consciousness called Apperception, or selective attention.

Rorschach — The Rorschach inkblot test is a method of psychological evaluation. It is a projective test associated with the Freudian school of thought. Psychologists use this test to try to probe the unconscious minds of their patients.

Questionnaire — A self-report method of data collection or clinical assessment method in which the individual being studied checks off items on a printed list, answers multiple-choice questions, or writes out answers to essay questions aimed at producing a selfdescription is called questionnaire.

Inference — Inference is the act or process of drawing a conclusion based solely on what one already knows.

Personality — Personality refers to the pattern of enduring characteristics that differentiates a person,

	the patterns of behaviors that make each individual unique.
Personality inventory	A self-report questionnaire by which an examinee indicates whether statements assessing habitual tendencies apply to him or her is referred to as a personality inventory.
Psychometric	Psychometric study is concerned with the theory and technique of psychological measurement, which includes the measurement of knowledge, abilities, attitudes, and personality traits. The field is primarily concerned with the study of differences between individuals
Attention	Attention is the cognitive process of selectively concentrating on one thing while ignoring other things. Psychologists have labeled three types of attention: sustained attention, selective attention, and divided attention.
Syndrome	The term syndrome is the association of several clinically recognizable features, signs, symptoms, phenomena or characteristics which often occur together, so that the presence of one feature indicates the presence of the others.
Neuropsychology	Neuropsychology is a branch of psychology that aims to understand how the structure and function of the brain relates to specific psychological processes.
Variable	A variable refers to a measurable factor, characteristic, or attribute of an individual or a system.
Negative affectivity	Negative affectivity is a personality variable that refers to a tendency to experience negative emotions across many different situations.
Family functioning	Family functioning is often defined in terms of the availability of two types of primary family resources: utilitarian and psychological.
Skinner	Skinner conducted research on shaping behavior through positive and negative reinforcement, and demonstrated operant conditioning, a technique which he developed in contrast with classical conditioning.
Child development	Scientific study of the processes of change from conception through adolescence is called child development.
Introspection	Introspection is the self report or consideration of one's own thoughts, perceptions and mental processes. Classic introspection was done through trained observers.
Empirical	Empirical means the use of working hypotheses which are capable of being disproved using observation or experiment.
Psychoanalytic	Freud's theory that unconscious forces act as determinants of personality is called psychoanalytic theory. The theory is a developmental theory characterized by critical stages of development.
Ego	In Freud's view the Ego serves to balance our primitive needs and our moral beliefs and taboos. Relying on experience, a healthy Ego provides the ability to adapt to reality and interact with the outside world.
Anna Freud	Anna Freud was a pioneer of child psychoanalysis. She popularized the notion that adolescence is a period that includes rapid mood fluctuation with enormous uncertainty about self.
Insight	Insight refers to a sudden awareness of the relationships among various elements that had previously appeared to be independent of one another.
Fixation	Fixation in abnormal psychology is the state where an individual becomes obsessed with an attachment to another human, animal or inanimate object. Fixation in vision refers to maintaining the gaze in a constant direction. .
Play therapy	Play therapy is often used to help the diagnostician to try to determine the cause of disturbed behavior in a child. Treatment therapists then used a type of systematic

desensitization or relearning therapy to change the disturbing behavior, either systematically or in less formal social settings.

Cognitive therapy
Cognitive therapy is a kind of psychotherapy used to treat depression, anxiety disorders, phobias, and other forms of mental disorder. It involves recognizing distorted thinking and learning how to replace it with more realistic thoughts and actions.

Modeling
A type of behavior learned through observation of others demonstrating the same behavior is modeling.

Conditioning
Conditioning describes the process by which behaviors can be learned or modified through interaction with the environment.

Classical conditioning
Classical conditioning is a simple form of learning in which an organism comes to associate or anticipate events. A neutral stimulus comes to evoke the response usually evoked by a natural or unconditioned stimulus by being paired repeatedly with the unconditioned stimulus.

Aversion therapy
Aversion therapy is a now largely discredited form of treatment in which the patient is exposed to a stimulus while simultaneously being hurt or made ill. The theory is that the patient will come to associate the stimulus with unpleasant sensations and will no longer seek it out.

Contingency management
Providing a supply of reinforcers to promote and maintain desired behaviors, and the prompt removal of reinforcers that maintain undesired behaviors is called contingency management.

Reinforcement
In operant conditioning, reinforcement is any change in an environment that (a) occurs after the behavior, (b) seems to make that behavior re-occur more often in the future and (c) that reoccurence of behavior must be the result of the change.

Stress inoculation
Use of positive coping statements to control fear and anxiety is a form of stress inoculation.

Behavioral rehearsal
Behavior therapy technique in which the client practices coping with troublesome or anxiety arousing situations in a safe and supervised situation is a behavioral rehearsal.

Behavioral pediatrics
A branch of behavioral medicine concerned with psychological aspects of childhood medical problems is called behavioral pediatrics.

Problem solving
An attempt to find an appropriate way of attaining a goal when the goal is not readily available is called problem solving.

Effect size
An effect size is the strength or magnitude of the difference between two sets of data or, in outcome studies, between two time points for the same population. (The degree to which the null hypothesis is false).

Cognition
The intellectual processes through which information is obtained, transformed, stored, retrieved, and otherwise used is cognition.

Generalization
In conditioning, the tendency for a conditioned response to be evoked by stimuli that are similar to the stimulus to which the response was conditioned is a generalization. The greater the similarity among the stimuli, the greater the probability of generalization.

Psychotherapy
Psychotherapy is a set of techniques based on psychological principles intended to improve mental health, emotional or behavioral issues.

Methylphenidate
Methylphenidate is a central nervous system (CNS) stimulant. It has a "calming" effect on many children who have ADHD, reducing impulsive behavior and the tendency to "act out", and helps them concentrate on schoolwork and other tasks. Adults who have ADHD often find that it increases their ability to focus on tasks and organize their lives. Brand names include Ritalin, and Concerta.

Ritalin	Ritalin, a methylphenidate, is a central nervous system stimulant. It has a "calming" effect on many children who have ADHD, reducing impulsive behavior and the tendency to "act out", and helps them concentrate on schoolwork and other tasks.
Antidepressant	An antidepressant is a medication used primarily in the treatment of clinical depression. They are not thought to produce tolerance, although sudden withdrawal may produce adverse effects. They create little if any immediate change in mood and require between several days and several weeks to take effect.
Tricyclic	Tricyclic antidepressants are a class of antidepressant drugs first used in the 1950s. They are named after the drugs' molecular structure, which contains three rings of atoms.
Tricyclic antidepressant	A tricyclic antidepressant is of a class of antidepressant drugs first used in the 1950s. They are named after the drugs' molecular structure, which contains three rings of atoms.
Psychosocial treatment	Psychosocial treatment focuses on social and cultural factors as well as psychological influences. These approaches include cognitive, behavioral, and interpersonal methods.
Community psychology	Community psychology is the study of how to use the principles of psychology to create communities of all sizes that promote mental health of their members.
Cystic fibrosis	Cystic fibrosis is an autosomal recessive hereditary disease of the exocrine glands. It affects the lungs, sweat glands and the digestive system. It causes chronic respiratory and digestive problems.
Psychosomatic	A psychosomatic illness is one with physical manifestations and perhaps a supposed psychological cause. It is often diagnosed when any known or identifiable physical cause was excluded by medical examination.
Stages	Stages represent relatively discrete periods of time in which functioning is qualitatively different from functioning at other periods.
Life span	Life span refers to the upper boundary of life, the maximum number of years an individual can live. The maximum life span of human beings is about 120 years of age. Females live an average of 6 years longer than males.
Developmental psychology	The branch of psychology that studies the patterns of growth and change occurring throughout life is referred to as developmental psychology.
Developmental psychopathology	Developmental psychopathology refers to the area of psychology that focuses on describing and exploring the developmental pathways of problems and disorders.
Community intervention	An approach to treating and preventing disorders by directing action at the organizational, agency, and community levels rather than at individuals is called a community intervention.
Ethnicity	Ethnicity refers to a characteristic based on cultural heritage, nationality characteristics, race, religion, and language.
Affect	A subjective feeling or emotional tone often accompanied by bodily expressions noticeable to others is called affect.
Principles of Behavior	Hull published Principles of Behavior, in 1943. His theory is characterized by very strict operationalization of variables and mathematical presentation. The essence of the theory can be summarized by saying that the response is a function of the strength of the habit times the strength of the drive. It is for this reason that Hull's theory is often referred to as drive theory.
Fisher	Fisher was a eugenicist, evolutionary biologist, geneticist and statistician. He has been described as "The greatest of Darwin's successors", and a genius who almost single-handedly created the foundations for modern statistical science inventing the techniques of maximum likelihood and analysis of variance.

Behavioral observation	A form of behavioral assessment that entails careful observation of a person's overt behavior in a particular situation is behavioral observation.
Psychological testing	Psychological testing is a field characterized by the use of small samples of behavior in order to infer larger generalizations about a given individual. The technical term for psychological testing is psychometrics.
Behavior therapy	Behavior therapy refers to the systematic application of the principles of learning to direct modification of a client's problem behaviors.
Etiology	Etiology is the study of causation. The term is used in philosophy, physics and biology in reference to the causes of various phenomena. It is generally the study of why things occur, or even the reasons behind the way that things act.
Norms	In testing, standards of test performance that permit the comparison of one person's score on the test to the scores of others who have taken the same test are referred to as norms.
Attention deficit/hype-activity disorder	Disorders of childhood and adolescence characterized by socially disruptive behaviors-either attentional problems or hyperactivity-that persist for at least six months are an attention deficit/hyperactivity disorder.
Brain	The brain controls and coordinates most movement, behavior and homeostatic body functions such as heartbeat, blood pressure, fluid balance and body temperature. Functions of the brain are responsible for cognition, emotion, memory, motor learning and other sorts of learning. The brain is primarily made up of two types of cells: glia and neurons.
Health psychology	The field of psychology that studies the relationships between psychological factors and the prevention and treatment of physical illness is called health psychology.
Socioeconomic	Socioeconomic pertains to the study of the social and economic impacts of any product or service offering, market intervention or other activity on an economy as a whole and on the companies, organization and individuals who are its main economic actors.
Clinical psychologist	A psychologist, usually with a Ph.D, whose training is in the diagnosis, treatment, or research of psychological and behavioral disorders is a clinical psychologist.
Adler	Adler argued that human personality could be explained teleologically, separate strands dominated by the guiding purpose of the individual's unconscious self ideal to convert feelings of inferiority to superiority (or rather completeness). The desires of the self ideal were countered by social and ethical demands.
Individual psychology	Alfred Adler's individual psychology approach views people as motivated by purposes and goals, being creators of their own lives .
Theory of planned behavior	The theory of planned behavior links attitudes and behavior. It holds that human action is guided by three kinds of considerations: Beliefs about the likely outcomes of the behavior and the evaluations of these outcomes; Beliefs about the normative expectations of others and motivation to comply with these expectations; and, Beliefs about the presence of factors that may facilitate or impede performance of the behavior and the perceived power of these factors.
Attitude	An enduring mental representation of a person, place, or thing that evokes an emotional response and related behavior is called attitude.
Counseling psychology	Counseling psychology is unique in its attention both to normal developmental issues and to problems associated with physical, emotional, and mental disorders.
Allport	Allport was a trait theorist. Those traits he believed to predominate a person's personality were called central traits. Traits such that one could be indentifed by the trait, were

referred to as cardinal traits. Central traits and cardinal traits are influenced by environmental factors.

Printed in the United States
101547LV00004B/16/A

9 781428 813182